IRISH WOMEN IN

LANCASHIRE

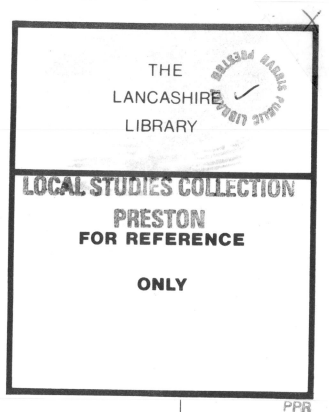

THE
LANCASHIRE
LIBRARY

LOCAL STUDIES COLLECTION

PRESTON
FOR REFERENCE

ONLY

Irish Women in Lancashire 1922–1960

Their Story

Sharon Lambert

Centre for North-West Regional Studies
University of Lancaster
2001
Series Editor: Jean Turnbull

Irish Women in Lancashire 1922–1960: Their Story

This volume is the 44th in a series published by the Centre for North-West Regional Studies at the University of Lancaster

Text copyright © Sharon Lambert 2001

Published by the Centre for North-West Regional Studies, University of Lancaster

Designed and typeset by Carnegie Publishing Ltd, Carnegie House, Chatsworth Road, Lancaster LA1 4SL

Printed and bound in the UK by The Cromwell Press, Trowbridge

British Library Cataloguing-in-Publication Data
A CIP catalogue record for this book is available from the British Library

ISBN 1–86220–110–2

Contents

For my mum, Maureen Deehan,
and in memory of my dad,
Barney Deehan

List of Illustrations

List of Tables

Foreword

The study of Irish immigrants in Britain has made striking progress in recent years, thanks to the work of several scholars, much of it collected in compendia like those edited by Roger Swift and Sheridan Gilley, *The Irish in Britain 1815–1939* (London, 1989), and *The Irish in Victorian Britain: the local dimension* (Dublin, 1999). Most of the generalisations still tend, however, to be based on source material in the public domain dealing mainly with the activities of male emigrants outside the home. Sharon Lambert's major contribution in this carefully crafted study of Irish women in Lancashire, 1922–1960, is reflected in her sub-title, 'Their Story'. It draws mainly on interviews with women themselves, seeking to push back the frontiers of our understanding by distilling the essence of their experience through their own eyes.

This type of material requires great sensitivity in dealing with the personalities involved. It also requires a rare sensitivity to one's own preconceptions. It requires the modesty and self-discipline to refrain from imposing our own ideological preferences on the subjects of the inquiry, and a capacity for seeing the world through their eyes as it really was for them, rather than through ours as we would have wished it to have been. It requires, in short, a combination of emotional with academic intelligence vouchsafed to few.

Sharon Lambert's refusal to treat the women as the mere objects of her own intellectual ambitions, her determination to let their world be seen outwards through their eyes, rather than imposing her own emotional or ideological needs onto them, as well as her candour in recounting her own background and life experiences, and her forthrightness about the possible flaws as well as the strengths in her oral interviewing techniques, all serve to reinforce confidence in her findings. As she rightly observes, no study can be entirely objective, but an awareness of one's own subjectivity should lead to a deeper understanding of the subject matter.

She is well aware of the limitations, in both statistical and human terms, of the sample of forty life histories on which she bases her conclusions. She does not make exaggerated claims for their 'statistical representativeness', but she does consciously seek out informants who 'reflect as many types of Irish emigrant women as possible'. The fact that many of her respondents were initially reluctant participants, believing they had nothing of significance to relate, is both poignant and reassuring.

Sharon Lambert's approach is not the only possible one. But in putting a human face on the emigrant experience, she rouses our interest from the outset. Her study makes an important contribution to our understanding of the history of Lancashire, of the history of Irish emigration, and of the history of women. Surely few readers will fail to be engaged by the compelling accounts of the challenges confronted, of loneliness and friendship, of loyalty and sacrifice, of joy and sorrow, recorded with such sensitivity in these pages.

J. J. Lee
Professor of History,
University College, Cork

Acknowledgements

This book is based on research undertaken for my PhD thesis but its origins go back much further, to my personal interest in Irish emigrant culture. My father was typical of the emigrant Irishmen who were immortalised in the ballad 'McAlpine's Fusileers'. He left rural Sligo to work on the farms, motorways and building sites of England but he brought his culture with him. I grew up listening to the songs and stories of Ireland and inherited his passion for Irish traditional music. Irish history was an obvious choice when I became a mature student and researching the lives of Irish women in Lancashire was a joy. My aim was to write an academic study in an accessible style and I hope that this book will appeal to a wide readership, especially to the Irish in Britain but also to anyone with an interest in the personal effects of emigration.

Many people have helped me along the path that led to writing this book. At Lancaster University I had the good fortune to meet two inspiring lecturers, Bill Fuge and John Walton, who encouraged and guided my interest in the history of the Irish in Britain. Grants from Lancaster University and the E.S.R.C. provided the financial means to undertake doctoral research and Professors Colin Pooley and John Walton provided the expert supervision required to complete it. The work of Dr Elizabeth Roberts inspired me to use oral history as my main research method. Dr Jean Turnbull, who smoothly managed the production of this book, was also a superb role model and confidante when I was undertaking postgraduate study.

Family influence is a major theme of this book and of my own life! I am grateful for the support, and plenty of diversions, which I received from having Mam, Terry, Paul, Chris, Danny and John Paul around me. Vinnie, Frankie and Alfie confirmed my theory that family ties are not broken by distance, only stretched.

Friends and family provided one source of illustrations for the book and I am grateful to Mary Walsh, Colm Mulligan, Josephine Haran, Alfie Deehan and Maureen Deehan for donating photographs. Mary Walsh provided so much material that she almost qualifies for co-authorship! Thanks are also due to Chris Beacock, Lancaster University Geography Dept. for providing the maps and to Sue Ashworth, Lancaster City Museum for the Lancaster street photograph. The illustrations from Irish archives were obtained by

Dr Barbara Walsh and I am indebted to her for so freely giving her valuable time and expert knowledge to secure them. I am also grateful to the generosity which she received from the following archivists: Michael Kavanagh, Kildare County Library, Newbridge; Grainne MacLochlainn, National Photographic Library, Dublin; the curators of the Fr Browne S.J. collection, Irish Picture Library, Dublin. I very much appreciate all the assistance which I received from Rose Morris, of the Irish World Heritage Centre and Irish Community Care, Manchester. Rose provided the photographs of Irish women at work and I am grateful to Nula Bradwell, Nora Higgins and the late Mary Gilligan for donating them to Irish Community Care and allowing them to be used here.

Unfortunately, I cannot name the people to whom I owe the most for producing this book because the forty wonderful women who so generously related their experiences were promised confidentiality. *Go raibh mile maith agat* for affording me the privilege of telling your story.

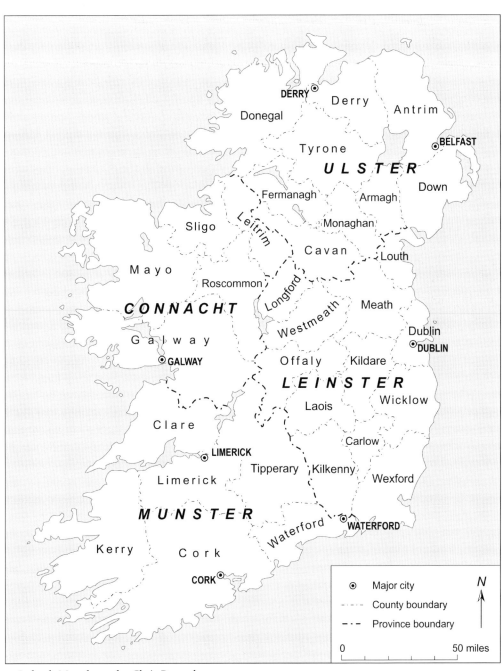

1. Ireland. Map drawn by Chris Beacock.

CUMBERLAND

WESTMORLAND

YORKSHIRE
(North Riding)

Kendal

Lune

Milnthorpe

Grange-over-Sands

Barrow-in-Furness

L A N C A S H I R E

Morecambe
Heysham
Lancaster

Wyre

YORKSHIRE
(West Riding)

Clitheroe

Blackpool

Ribble

Preston

Accrington

Blackburn

Irish

Sea

Rochdale

Wigan

Ashton under Lyne

St. Helens

Manchester

Liverpool

Stockport

DERBYSHIRE

Mersey

CHESHIRE

0   5   10 miles

2. Lancashire (pre-1973 boundary changes). Map drawn by Chris Beacock.

CHAPTER ONE

Introduction

In this book, Irish women talk about their lives in Ireland and Lancashire between 1922 and 1960. Their life-histories were recorded during interviews with the author and most of the women viewed their lives as unremarkable. Their testimonies, however, tell another story. Most of these women left Southern Ireland as young, single women, between the ages of 15 and 24, to settle in the country from which the new Irish state had only recently gained independence. Not only did they face the everyday social and economic difficulties of adapting to life in a new country, the post-colonial relationship of Ireland and Britain also burdened them with a psychological barrier to assimilation. As Maura, who came to Morecambe in 1945 to work as a chambermaid, said: 'You were sort o' taught to hate England and then sent here'. Yet, quietly, in their own view 'unremarkably', they got on with their lives and made the best of their opportunities in Lancashire.

The story of Irish women's lives in Lancashire makes an important contribution to the history of the Irish in Britain. From the late nineteenth century, the numbers of Irish women in Britain have roughly equalled and often surpassed those of Irish men but their story has been hidden in general studies of Irish immigration based on male experiences. Research on the history of the Irish in Britain has also been concentrated on the nineteenth century, when sectarianism and conflicts between the Irish and English working-classes were common features of several North-West towns.[1] General studies of British immigration in the twentieth century tend to concentrate on the more visible problems faced by Black and Asian immigrants and little attention is paid to the Irish. Very little research has been published on the Irish in twentieth-century Britain or on Irish women in any period.

The history of the Irish in Britain has usually been written from the outside, from sources in which the Irish were perceived as a social problem. The studies of Irish men in the nineteenth century were largely compiled from sources which reflected British upper and middle-class alarm concerning the mass-urbanisation of Victorian Britain and the heavy concentration of destitute Irish people in northern towns, particularly during and after the Irish Famine. Oral history has been adopted as the prime source of information for this study, so as to enable Irish

3. Irish men in Lancaster, 1961. Despite half of Irish emigrants being women, the familiar image of the Irish in Britain is that of Irish men (the author's father is pictured, second row, third from right).

women's history to be written, as far as possible, from their own perspective.

This book covers the period from 1922 to 1960 and it is confined to women who left Southern Ireland and settled in Lancashire. These dates were chosen because 1922 marked the beginning of Irish independence and 1960 marked the end of a period of high emigration from Southern Ireland. In 1961, net emigration declined and the population began to grow.[2] Up until the 1960s the new Irish state remained a mainly rural, Catholic and conservative society with high levels of emigration. Emigrants from Southern Ireland were chosen in order to explore the effects which Catholicism and Ireland's post-colonial relationship with Britain had on their experiences of emigration to Britain. A regional study of Irish women in Lancashire was chosen because the existing oral history material provides details of Lancashire women's lives which can be compared with the experiences of the Irish women in this study.[3]

Before proceeding further, it is necessary to explain the use of the terms 'Southern Ireland' and 'emigration'. The complicated political history of Ireland and Britain has resulted in several name changes on the island of Ireland. From the Act of Union, which was passed in 1800 and was effective from the 1st January 1801, Ireland became part of the United Kingdom and was subject to direct rule from Westminster. Ireland was partitioned under the Government of Ireland Act of 1920. Six counties in the province of Ulster were called Northern Ireland and remained in the United Kingdom and the other 26 counties of Ireland received dominion status and were named the Irish Free State. In 1937 the Irish constitution changed the Free State's name to Eire [Ireland] and in 1949 these 26 counties became the Irish Republic.

Although it has never been an official name, Southern Ireland is commonly used to refer to the 26 counties which are now independent from Britain. It is often used in this book because it provides a convenient name for the geographical area in any time period and thus avoids the possibility of confusion from constantly changing the collective name of the 26 counties when referring to different years. In this book: where the word 'Ireland' is used, it refers to the whole island; 'Northern Ireland' refers to the six counties which remain in the United Kingdom; and 'Southern Ireland' refers to the twenty six counties which now constitute the Irish Republic.

Use of the word 'emigration', to describe the movement of Irish women to Britain, goes against the trend in some recent works to refer to Irish 'migration'. When *The Irish World Wide* series was being compiled its editor, Patrick O'Sullivan, directed the contributors to avoid using: 'those emotionally-freighted words "emigrant" and "immigrant"' and advised them to use instead: 'the more neutral word "migrant"'.[4] One contributor to the series, Donald Harman Akenson, warns against using the terms 'emigrant' and 'immigrant' because they are 'confusing'.[5] O'Sullivan's main objective for prescribing the use of 'migration' rather than 'emigration' is not simply to aid clarity in the text, he is concerned about the implications of focussing the narrative upon nation states. This point has some relevance when considering the history and politics of Ireland and Britain. Within the British Isles, international boundaries were technically non-existent throughout the nineteenth and early-twentieth centuries and since 1922 they have existed between Southern Ireland and the United Kingdom, which includes Northern Ireland, but not between Northern Ireland and Britain. It is curious, however, that neither O'Sullivan nor Akenson have any difficulties with using the term 'Irish diaspora', which implies that the dispersal of Irish people originally belonged to one nation.[6] Had Northern Irish women been included in the study, the chosen vocabulary might have been different but, for the purposes of this book, the word 'emigration' is justifiable. Southern Irish women who moved to live in Britain between 1922 and 1960 left one nation to inhabit another. During the years covered by this study, 'emigration' was also the traditional historical and contemporary term that was most often used to describe population movement from the whole island, including Northern Ireland. The main reason for choosing the term 'emigration' rather than 'migration' is that the women of the oral history sample generally referred to themselves as 'emigrants'. Describing the women in terms which they used themselves is consistent with the important objective of writing this book as much as possible from the perspective of Irish emigrant women.

The design of the oral history

I have written this final section of the introduction in the uncharacteristic, but appropriate, first person because one of the main things which I learned from setting up this oral history was that, despite my initial efforts at maintaining objectivity, it was a very subjective exercise. I have since come to the conclusion that this is unavoidable, particularly in interviewing, when the relationship between the interviewer and respondent undoubtedly affects the quality of the information which is obtained. Acknowledgement of the fact that a subjective relationship exists within interviews should not necessarily alarm historians. On the contrary, an awareness of this knowledge should have a positive effect on the discourse, and consequently the historical evidence, which is obtained through personal interviews

Informants

Numbers of oral history informants can range from Paul Thompson's ambitiously constructed quota sample of five hundred old people for his book The Edwardians, to the single voice of Paddy Fahey, whose life story was recorded by Bernadette Halpin for *The Irish in London*.[7] Since oral testimony is an essentially qualitative source of historical information, the number of informants is, in my opinion, of less significance to the study's value than their characteristics. I wanted to interview as many women as time would allow, simply because I wanted to explore a diversity of experiences within the oral history. My initial arbitrary target of fifty women proved to be over ambitious and the final sample contained forty life-histories.

I was not concerned with obtaining a statistically representative sample, not only because of the difficulties which the sheer logistics of such an enterprise would have posed, but because I believe that it is impossible. The most basic reason why oral history respondents cannot be deemed to be 'representative', of whatever group of society in whichever place or time period, is that they have survived. They can at best, therefore, only statistically represent the members of that group who are still living at the time of interview. In any case, for the purposes of this research, details of the exact numbers of women who left Southern Ireland and located in Lancashire during the forty years under investigation are not available.

Whilst I could make no claims of statistical representativeness, I made efforts to minimise any bias in order to make the sample reflect as many types of Irish emigrant women as possible. The main categories which I wanted to include in the sample were women: of all economic classes; from various regions in Southern Ireland; from urban and rural backgrounds; of different religions; married and single; from a variety of occupations, including nuns; and returned emigrants. I decided not to target the most fruitful sources of informants, such as Irish associations and Catholic churches, since it would have biased the sample towards women who were immersed in Irish Catholic culture in Britain. I was interested in the extent to which Irish women chose to maintain Irish cultural links after emigration but in order to ascertain this it was also necessary to include those women who rejected, or were apathetic about, Irish cultural activities. In the belief that local newspapers attract a broader social readership than the national press, I advertised for volunteers in twenty eight regional newspapers, covering all areas of Lancashire and the Irish Republic. I also placed advertisements in *The Irish Post*, a newspaper serving the Irish in Britain, and *Ireland's Own*, a weekly magazine of interest to older Irish readers. The outcome of this was, however, disappointing as I only received three letters of response from readers of *The Sligo Champion, Ireland's Own* and the *Lancashire Evening Post*.

Most respondents were eventually found through personal contacts and they were often initially reluctant and had to be persuaded to 'volunteer'. A common misconception amongst potential informants was that their life-histories 'would not be interesting enough' to contribute to the study. I seriously underestimated both the length of time and the effort which was required in recruiting informants. Women whom I had already interviewed proved to be a source of further informants. They would tell me the names of other Irish women and often persuade reluctant friends to participate in the research. The sample was not, however, made up only of Irish women who knew each other. Many of my own friends and acquaintances were also informed of my wish to contact older Irish women and they provided access to potential informants, sometimes from within their family, their neighbourhood or their workplace, or through mentioning my research to someone else who knew of a woman who might be suitable. Some informants were even recruited after myself, or someone acting on my behalf, had approached them upon overhearing their Irish accent.

Although the process of gathering informants for this study was often slow and laborious, it did succeed in its intention of avoiding the bias towards women involved with the Irish community in

Britain. The sample also contained the preferred diversity of social classes, occupations, geographical origins and destinations. Three emigrants who returned to live in Ireland were also included. The sample was less satisfactory in its range of religious affiliations since it comprised thirty nine Catholics and only one Baptist. It was not, however, biased towards practising Catholics as it would have been if Catholic churches had been targetted for respondents. Also, a majority of Catholic informants was to be expected given their predominance in Southern Irish society. In 1961, almost 95% of people in the Republic of Ireland were Catholics. More details on the respondents are given in the next chapter and in the biographies in the appendix.

The Interviews

There are many debates and conflicts of opinion amongst historians about the best methods of oral history interviewing and they begin with the selection of interviewers. In his book, *Listening to History*, Trevor Lummis discusses the ambivalence which many oral history practitioners have shown towards using informed interviewers. In his opinion, oral histories generated by 'ordinary people', might be more democratic than those collected by an elite group of academics but they are, nevertheless, academically inferior to oral histories conducted by trained historians. His conclusion is that: 'oral evidence collected within the framework of certain methodological guidelines and an informed historical imagination is a more useful and better historical source than ill-informed practice'.[8] Whilst I would agree that it is beneficial for the interviewer, or at least someone directing the oral history collection, to have a degree of historical knowledge in order to focus the information received and place it in the correct historical context, I would not go along with Lummis' inherent presumption that all trained oral historians are necessarily socially remote from their interviewees. The historical profession in Britain might still be disproportionately dominated by white, middle-class males but it is not exclusively comprised of such a narrow section of society. Women, the working-class and ethnic minorities are just a few examples of the social varieties which exist amongst historians in common with the wider British population.

Debate also exists amongst historians about the best ways to conduct interviews. Paul Thompson warns against the interviewer becoming too familiar with respondents because he believes that the information then received will be more inhibited and more likely to conform to social norms.[9] I found that this view was reflected by several social historians during discussions which I had with experienced oral history practitioners prior to starting my interviews. Nevertheless, I am not convinced by it and I did not follow this particular directive when interviewing. Thompson has in this case, I believe, demonstrated a similar degree of elitism to Trevor Lummis, in assuming that all trained oral historians are outside the social group of all interviewees.

I am more impressed by the methods of feminist historians such as Karen Olsen and Linda Shopes who emphasise the importance of a shared dialogue between the interviewer and interviewee. They found their own informants to be most forthcoming when they revealed information about themselves. Acutely conscious of the class difference between themselves and their informants, Olsen and Shopes sought to emphasise other common areas between themselves and their interviewees in an attempt to make the interviews more equal.[10] I conducted my interviews with the same intentions as Olsen and Shopes, but from the opposite perspective. I was more conscious of the similarities than the differences between myself and the interviewees and I saw my background as an asset to interviewing Irish women in Lancashire. I entered higher education as a mature student and being an historian was just one, relatively recent, aspect of my life. I also had other life-experiences with which many of my informants could identify: I was born into a Catholic working-class family and grew up on a council estate in Lancaster; my mother worked in numerous factories, cafes and shops to support the family wage; my father left a small farm in Co. Sligo in the 1950s and laboured on various motorways and building sites in England; I had been a clerical assistant, a psychiatric nurse and a care officer in a hostel for the mentally ill; I was the wife of a lorry driver and the mother of three sons. Several of the interviewees who were living in Lancaster already knew me socially, either through my parents or because I had attended the same schools as their children, and they regarded me in this light, as a social equal, rather than as an academic. It was interesting, and pleasing, that this perception of me was also apparent amongst the women whom I had never met before their interviews. This point is illustrated in the following dialogue from the transcript of the interview with Maureen, who was born into an Irish family in Wigan in 1923, and has lived on a small farm in Co. Sligo since her marriage in 1951. She was having difficulty in remembering a song which her mother used to sing[11] and asked me if my father had ever sung it:

> Would your father be singing that song, it was er ... O'Donnell you shot my husband'? You know, it was about when they shot them at the, er ...?

> SL: Can you remember any of the air of it? How did it go?

Yeah, it was about, you know, Phoenix Park where they shot Burke ... and Hare? Burke and who was the name?

SL: Cavendish, Lord Cavendish was shot and Burke.

Cavendish, yes! And then they got the ones ...?

SL: The Invincibles.

Yeah, that's it! Ye have it all off!

SL: It's Irish history I'm doing.

Are ye really? There's not many younger ones in England hearing that now is there?

Maureen had responded to the letter which I placed in *The Sligo Champion* and I met her for the first time on the day of the interview. As with all the interviewees, I had spent a period of time chatting in her house before starting the interview. I found that these introductory chats were necessary in order to relax both the informants and myself and minimise the strangeness of such a situation, where the women were being asked to recount personal details of their lives to a virtual stranger. Although I had included in the newspaper letter, and our correspondence before the interview, the fact that I was an historian, this was not an important aspect of my personality in Maureen's view. Her main perception of me was that I was a woman from working-class Lancashire with a Sligo father, features which I had in common with her. My academic persona was so irrelevant to her that being reminded of it during the interview surprised her.

Most of the interviews were conducted in the respondents' homes, with three taking place in my home. I took steps to minimise the 'strangeness' of the interviews and break down any potential barriers, such as shyness or awkwardness. Before each interview, I spent time chatting to the women and answering any questions they wished to ask me. I found that this made the interaction more balanced; I expected the interviewees to record their lives in detail so it was only fair that I should allow them to get to know some details about me as well. These pre-interview discussions were also necessary to establish a relationship of trust between us. I did not usually leave straight after the recorded interview but spent another hour or so in conversation. The majority of the recorded interviews were two hours long and I spent, on average, about four hours in each interviewee's house. Although my methods were contrary to those of some historians, who argue against familiarity in interviews, I am satisfied that they were successful in empowering the respondents, and creating a relationship of trust and equality between us, which was necessary in order for them to disclose information about intimate areas of their life histories. The nature of individual oral histories determines the optimum degree of familiarity between interviewees and respondents. If this history was only concerned with descriptive memories of less intimate areas of experience, the relationship between myself and the interviewees would have been less important. In this case, however, I do not believe that my respondents would have been as forthcoming with details of private and personal experiences, such as their sexual behaviour and their feelings regarding personal relationships, if they had not trusted me. In order to trust me, they needed to know more about me than the bare fact that I was an interested historian.

The interview structure

I only asked a few specific questions, regarding date of birth, birth-place etc., at the beginning of each interview. After these initial questions, I adopted a flexible approach and asked respondents to recount their lives in chronological order, in the hope that they would emphasise the areas which they felt to have been most important in their lives. After several interviews some definite themes had emerged. The family, religion and national identity were topics which all of the women prioritised within their life stories and talked about the most. I subsequently designed the study around these themes. This method fulfilled an important aim of ensuring that the respondents contributed not only to the content, but also to the design, of the study.

Some steps have been taken to preserve the anonymity of the respondents as much as possible in the writing of the book. They have been identified only by first name pseudonyms and their birthplace is only given at large town or county level. The first names of their relatives, when they have been cited, have also been changed.

Notes

1. A few select examples are: Walter L. Arnstein, 'The Murphy riots: A Victorian Dilemma', *Victorian Studies*, Sept. 1985, pp. 51–71; F. Neal, 'The Birkenhead Garibaldi Riots of 1862', *Historic Society of Lancashire and Cheshire*, vol. 131, 1981, pp. 87–111; Frank Neal, 'Manchester Origins of the English Orange Order', *Manchester Region History Review*, vol. iv, no. 2, 1990–91; Frank Neal, 'English-Irish Conflict in the North West of England: Economics, Racism, Anti-Catholicism or Simple Xenophobia?', *North West Labour History*, no. 16, 1991/92, pp. 14–25.

2. P. J. Drudy, *Irish Studies 5: Ireland and Britain since 1922*, 1986, p. 115.

3. Elizabeth Roberts, *Social and Family Life in Preston, 1880–1940*. Transcribed interviews from a Northwest oral history project, Lancaster University, Lancaster University Library; Elizabeth Roberts. *A Woman's Place: An Oral History of Working-Class Women 1890–1940*, 1984; Elizabeth Roberts, *Women and Families: An Oral History, 1940–1970*, 1995.

4. Patrick O'Sullivan, *The Irish World Wide, Vol. 4, Irish Women and Irish Migration*, 1995, p. 2.

5. Donald Harman Akensen, 'The historiography of the Irish in the United States', in Patrick O'Sullivan (ed.), *The Irish World Wide, Vol. 2, The Irish in the New Communities*, 1992, p. 100.

6. Patrick O'Sullivan, *The Irish World Wide, Vol. 4, Irish Women and Irish Migration*, 1995, p. 1.

7. Paul Thompson, *The Edwardians*, 1975; Paddy Fahey, *The Irish in London*, 1992.

8. Trevor Lummis, *Listening to History*, p. 23.

9. Paul Thompson, 'Problems of Method in Oral history', *Oral History*, 1973, pp. 20–21.

10. K. Olsen and L. Shopes, 'Crossing boundaries, building bridges: doing oral history amongst working-class women and men', in S. Gluck and D. Patei (eds), *Women's Words*, 1991, pp. 189–204.

11. Incidentally, the song is 'Pat O'Donnell' and it can be found in: Colm O'Lochlainn, *The Complete Irish Street Ballads*, 1984, pp. 210–211.

CHAPTER TWO

Explaining female emigration from Ireland

The extent of emigration from Ireland

The impact of emigration on Ireland's demographic structure has been most significant since the time of the Great Famine, which began in 1845. In the middle of the nineteenth century, whilst the population of all other European countries was rising, Ireland's population declined. The decline was followed by consistent stagnation in the twentieth century and in 1961 Ireland's population was just over half of what it had been in 1841.[1] Apart from the Great Famine years of the late 1840s, when probably as many people died as fled from Ireland, the dramatic population decline was largely due to emigration. Ireland was the only country in Europe where emigration was consistently greater than the excess of births over deaths and it had the highest emigration rate in Europe until 1960.[2]

Geographical origins of Irish emigrants

Before the Famine, emigrants tended to be from the relatively more prosperous areas of Ireland; from the more fertile lands of the south and east and from Ulster, particularly when the traditional domestic linen industry was beginning to suffer from competition from the mills in England.[3] After the Famine, emigration became more widespread over the whole country and by the end of the nineteenth century most emigrants were increasingly leaving the poorer and less industrialised counties, especially those in Connaught. This pattern continued in the twentieth century.[4]

Southern Ireland's population declined at a far greater rate than that of the more industrialised Northern Ireland (table 2.1). In 1951, 23% of the Irish Republic's employed population worked in industry; 36% in services; and 41% in agriculture. In Northern Ireland, 44% of employed people worked in industry; 38% in services; and 18% in agriculture.[5] The 1961 census classified 60% of the Irish Republic's population as living in rural areas and population loss was heaviest from the country areas. The 1950s witnessed a massive exodus of people when the Republic's economy declined to such an extent that male agricultural employment fell by 35% and women's by 12%.[6]

Between 1951 and 1961, more than 400,000 people left Southern Ireland, most of them heading for Britain.[7] It has been estimated that 'four out of every five children born in Ireland between 1931 and 1941 emigrated in the 1950s'.[8] In the 1961 census, twenty two of the independent twenty six counties recorded smaller populations than they had in 1926. The eastern counties of Dublin, Meath, Kildare and Louth were the only ones whose populations had increased after the first forty years of independence.[9]

Geographical origins of the women in this study

The majority of the oral history sample conformed to the dominant pattern of emigrants originating mainly from the western counties of Ireland.[10] Two of the women were born in England. Maureen was born to an Irish family in Wigan and settled in Sligo when she married. Agnes, who was born in Coventry, moved back to her parent's birthplace in Co. Roscommon when she was less than a year old and left Roscommon for Lancashire nineteen years later. As she perceived this second move as emigration, she can be added to the total of Roscommon emigrants. This makes a total of 25 women (64% of the sample of 39 emigrants), originating from the seven western counties of Clare, Donegal, Galway, Kerry, Mayo, Roscommon and Sligo. Additionally, 30 women, or 77% of the emigrant sample, originated from rural areas. The relatively high number of five emigrants from Dublin does not, however, reflect the general pattern of Irish emigration which was much greater from western and rural counties during this period.

Gender distribution of emigrants

The extent of post-Famine emigration from Southern Ireland was indeed remarkable but the main feature which sets Southern Irish emigration apart from that of other European countries is the high proportion of female emigrants. The numbers of women who left Ireland are anomalous when compared with migration statistics for other European countries which are usually dominated by males.[11] Between 1871 and 1971, there was a small excess of female over male emigrants from the 26 counties of Southern Ireland. For the whole century there was a yearly average of 15,707 male, and 15,983 female, emigrants.[12] For the years relevant to this study, more women than men emigrated except during the years of World War Two and the 1950s. Many Irish men either joined the British forces or found employment in Britain during World War Two but emigration of Irish women was restricted during this period. Irish females under

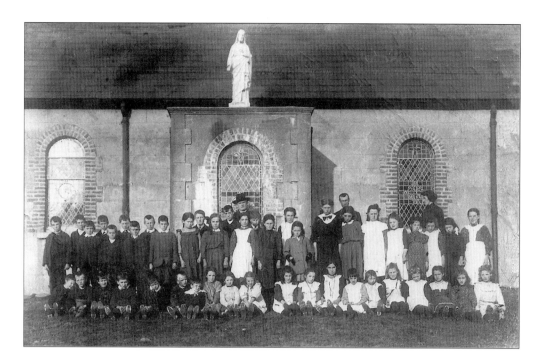

4. Largan
National School,
Co. Sligo, 1913.
At least 37 of the
46 children
pictured here are
known to have
emigrated on
reaching
adulthood.
Reproduced
courtesy of Alfie
Deehan who
gathered this
information from
the late
Mary-Anne
Deehan.

the age of twenty two, for example, were only allowed to emigrate if they were going to train or work as nurses, teachers or midwives. Only women over the age of twenty two were allowed to go to work in British factories.[13] The higher number of male than female emigrants during the 1950s is mainly attributable to the massive decline in male agricultural employment in the Irish Republic during that decade. The years when the oral history sample emigrants left Ireland range from 1910 to 1965, with the bulk of women emigrating in the 1930s, '40s and '50s.[14]

Age distribution of Irish emigrants

During the crisis years of the Famine, family emigration of adults and children was most common. Family emigration largely declined in the post-Famine years and young adults between the ages of 15 and 24 formed the majority of emigrants. This young adult age group continued to predominate among the emigrants who left Ireland throughout the years covered in this book but there were some gendered variations in the pattern during certain years. Between 1924 and 1939, half of all Irish emigrants were in the 15–24 category. This was also the case during the years of the Second World War but emigration (mainly to Britain) among older males increased during the war years whilst female emigrants remained mainly young. Between 1939 and 1952, intending Irish emigrants to Britain were required to obtain travel and employment permits or travel identity cards. The age-distribution of the recipients of these documents, and also those of passport recipients, shows that female emigrants generally tended to be younger than male emigrants. Between 1943 and 1951, almost half of the Irish males who received an official travel document were under the age of 25 whilst the comparative proportion of females was nearly 70%.[15] During the high emigration years of the 1950s, family emigration increased and the numbers of older male emigrants decreased. The average age of female emigrants remained younger than males for the years concerned in this study and comparatively fewer older women than men emigrated.[16] Almost 81% of the oral history sample emigrated from Ireland between the ages of 15 and 24.[17] In common with most of their contemporary female Irish emigrants, the majority of the oral history sample left Ireland as young, single women. Only two of them emigrated as infants and only four emigrated after they were married.

Irish emigration to Lancashire

In the 19th century the majority of emigrants from Ireland went to the United States, with a lesser number going to Britain, Canada and Australia. From the 1920s, after the United States imposed quota restrictions on immigrants, Britain began to replace the U.S.A. as the main destination of Irish emigrants.[18]

By the 1920s there was already a strong tradition of Irish settlement in Lancashire. North west England was one of the three main areas of Britain to which huge numbers of Irish people fled during and after the Great Famine of 1845–49. London and Scotland were the other major destinations during this period. In 1851, 41% of all the Irish-born residents of England and Wales were in the two north-west counties of Lancashire and Cheshire.[19] Whilst London received the highest numbers of Irish people, an Irish presence was most visible in Liverpool, where 22.3% of the total population was Irish-born in 1851. In the same year 13.1% of the population of Manchester and Salford; 10.6% of Stockport; 7.4% of Preston; and 7.3% of Bolton were Irish-born.[20]

During the twentieth century, Lancashire continued to be a traditional area of Irish settlement in England and its Irish population figures were second only to London. In 1961, the total Irish-born population of London was 162,141 and in Lancashire it was 107,527. From the 1930s, however, the Irish were moving in increasing numbers to the new industrial areas of England; to towns and cities such as Birmingham, Coventry and Leicester in the Midlands, and Luton and Bedford in the South-East.[21]

Compared with the wider Irish emigrant population, the women in the oral history sample have been found to be fairly typical in age and marital status at emigration, and in their geographical origins. These statistics, however, provide little insight into the emigrants' lives; as Robert Kennedy essentially pointed out 'individuals – not aggregate rates – move, marry, and have babies'. [22]

Why did Irish women leave?

Between 1926 and 1961, an estimated 882,196 people emigrated from Southern Ireland.[23] The majority of them were heading for Britain and slightly less than half of them were women. Why did so many women leave Ireland? Why did they go to particular destinations? The traditional view that 'the principle and immediate cause of emigration remains economic'[24] is now being revised because it was based only on male emigrant experiences and the probability that women left Ireland for social as much as economic reasons is now being acknowledged. Oral testimonies from emigrants provide a valuable source of evidence for uncovering the reasons behind Irish women's emigration.

If they had not offered the information unprompted, the respondents were specifically asked to explain the circumstances of their emigration: how and why they left Ireland, and how they felt at the time. The traditional economic explanation was often cited as the impetus for emigration, especially amongst women from poorer rural backgrounds. Small family farm incomes were unable to sustain all the children as they left school and women who worked on them after they left school expressed an awareness of being a financial burden to their family and a sense of their childhood being prolonged by not being financially independent and having to ask for money to buy new clothes or to go to dances. Domestic service was often the only local employment alternative for women who grew up on small farms and whose families could not afford to extend their education beyond primary level:

> In the towns or the villages, being the kitchen maid for the publican or the person with the business, that was the typical job. The girl would be in the back kitchen doing the chores, and maybe up at seven in the morning looking after the children, and stayed in that background and wasn't seen out, you know. It was like the Victorian days here [England] really. That would be about all there was for girls, you know. Unless you went to Dublin, unless you went to the cities. (Breda, b. 1928, Co. Roscommon)

Siobhan was born in Co. Donegal in 1938 and she was one of the

youngest respondents. Her recollections show the gruelling conditions which many farm servants had to endure in Ireland as late as
the 1950s:

> I went to work for farmers. You were hired by the six month and I got
> £30 for six month. You didn't get paid till the end o' the six months.
> You got up in the morning at 6 o'clock to milk the cows and feed the
> calves and hens. And then you gone in and made breakfast for the working
> men and washed up and then done the beds and all the bedrooms. Then
> by that time it was time to make the dinner for the farmer and the
> workmen and everybody. When dinnertime was finished you washed up
> and cleared away, washed the floor again – the kitchen floor was washed
> three times a day, the farmer's wife was a bit of a fanatic – and fed the
> animals again, like the young calves and the chicken and the dog and
> all. And then at 3 o'clock you took tea and sandwiches to whichever part
> o' the farm the men were working in. You walked to the field and you
> come back, and by that time it was time to start milking again and getting
> all the things ready and making the evening tea. You were steady at it
> from six in the morning to six at night. And that was seven days a week!
> You got just time off on Sunday, to get washed and changed, and you
> had to ride a bicycle four or five miles to Mass. And when you come
> back again, you got straight into your working clothes and started to
> make the dinner ... You had two nights off on a Tuesday and Friday
> but ye had to be in by 10 o'clock and it was 3 or 4 miles to get home to
> see me family ... I done that for eighteen month. I done three six-months.
> (Siobhan, b. 1938, Co. Donegal)

It was not only in large houses and farms that women worked in
domestic service and the conditions were not always as harsh as
those endured by Siobhan. Several women recalled living and working on neighbouring small farms after leaving school and such jobs
were usually arranged for them between their parents and the
prospective employer. Annie was born on a small farm in Cavan in
1929 and she was the second eldest of ten children. After leaving
school at fourteen she went to keep house for two bachelor farmers
in her own locality. She found the work to be easier than the tasks
she had done at home and the farmers were kind to her but she
went back home after ten months because she missed her family:

> The farmers, when they'd have done their work, they'd come in and visit
> us ... One night I had gone to bed and I could hear one of them saying
> to me mum: "Annie won't be old enough, you wouldn't let her go to
> work, would you, yet?" And me mother said: "Well you'll have to ask
> Annie herself." So I heard this and I thought it would be wonderful, you
> know, to get away to a house where there were no other children. It just

shows how naive I was! So I volunteered that I would go and be their housekeeper. The two men were lovely men. They were only in their thirties but at the time I thought they were old men. And they were very, very kind to me. They were out working hard all day – and it was very unusual to find a house locked up you see – so they wanted somebody in the house to keep the fire going, to wash the dishes and to prepare the meals. There wasn't any task in the house that I couldn't do and I just loved it. They were so surprised that I was able to do all these things but it was because I came from a big family and we automatically did all this, you know. It was no big deal. And I even milked the cows, you know … After a few weeks the novelty wore off and I began to feel very homesick … I used to go home every Sunday and me father would walk back with me. But I was very, very loyal. I would never say I was homesick because I knew they would be upset. So I always made it sound like I was so happy but deep down I was very, very unhappy. (Annie, b. 1929, Co. Cavan)

Annie remained in this job for ten months because she viewed her own personal happiness as less important than upsetting her family.

The respondents generally viewed domestic service as the least attractive employment option for women in Ireland during the time of their youth. Not only did domestic servants often have to work hard for long hours, they had also little status in Irish society. Philomena was born in 1917 in Co. Mayo and she recalled how her younger sister's employer forbade her from associating with a friend who was a servant:

My sister worked in the Post Office in Killala and she trained there. And one of her best friends from the village was a domestic servant and she had to live in. The two of them used to go out socially together and they'd cycle home together on their day off. And my sister's boss, Mrs. O'Hara, said to her: "It's come to my notice that you've been associating with a domestic servant. You have not to do it anymore, you are working in the Post Office!" (Philomena, b. 1917, Co. Mayo)

For all the respondents who worked in domestic service, it was their first experience of paid employment and they were usually between the ages of fourteen and sixteen. It was undertaken through economic necessity and the women left when they found alternative employment. Several of the respondents from rural areas in the western counties could not even find work in farm or domestic service and left Ireland without ever being able to secure paid employment.

The women who were born in or near urban areas had comparatively more local job opportunies and all of them worked for a time in Ireland before emigrating. Some of the respondents also migrated from rural areas to work in Irish towns, several of them moving across the border to Northern Ireland. Most of these were women from Donegal who worked in factories in Derry. Unlike domestic service, factory work in Ireland carried no social stigma for the respondents and the women who undertook it reported that they enjoyed it. Even within the towns, women from poorer backgrounds were restricted in their choice of employment. Shop work, for example, was often only open to those girls whose parents could afford to keep them while they were training, as was nursing. All of the respondents who were trained nurses undertook their training in England because, unlike in Ireland, they had no fees to pay and were paid a wage whilst training.

Lily left school at fourteen and her parents could not afford to send her to secondary school or into retail apprenticeship. Nevertheless, she was able to obtain work in three shops in Athlone before she emigrated. She attributed this to being a Protestant; the shopkeepers who employed her were also Protestants. Her recollections illustrate a sense of loss and isolation amongst the minority Protestant community in Ireland after independence:

> When I left school at fourteen I was as thick as they come ... But I wasn't out of school long when an elderly, disabled Protestant woman was looking for somebody. She had a little shop. In the good old days they had a sweet factory and they had a good little business and they ran it very well. Of course their money came from when the British were there. But now she was an elderly lady and things had gone all the way down. It was now the Free State and things had quite changed – this was about 1942 ... I spent three happy years there ... Then I went to work for a man who had another little shop and it was nearer home ... It was kind of boring because you sold nothing only cigarettes and ice-cream ... but right across was the biggest shop in town and he [the owner] was another Protestant ... One day I just happened to be passing by their place and he came running out – He was a marvellous businessman but he employed Catholics as well as Protestants, there was no distinction with him. He needed people and there weren't enough Protestants around – He ran out on the path one day and he said: "Now Miss Lamb, I hear you're working for Jack Egan. How much is he giving you?" I said he was giving me a pound and he said: "I'll give you thirty shillings if you come and work for me." It was the best thing I ever did. (Lily, b. 1929, Athlone)

Lily's recollection is interesting, not just for its evidence of self-help amongst the Protestant community in Athlone but also for its insight into how Protestants felt after the foundation of the Free State. Lily described the years before independence as 'the good old days' and commented that after that 'things had gone all the way down.' Such sentiments were shared by many Protestants, who left Southern Ireland in proportionately greater numbers than Catholics after independence. Catholics had always been predominant in Southern Ireland but their comparative dominance quickly increased after 1922. In 1911 Catholics constituted almost 90% of Southern Ireland's population and by 1961 this figure had risen to nearly 95%.[25]

In contrast to Lily's perception, that the economic decline in post-independence Ireland was due to British withdrawal, the majority view amongst Southern Irish people at the time was that Britain was still to blame for emigration. Joan was the fifth of twelve children born into a small farming family in Co Mayo. All twelve children emigrated, the eldest four to America and the rest to Britain. Joan reluctantly emigrated for economic reasons in 1933, when she was eighteen, and she blamed British policy for forcing her to leave:

> I had anger against me family for allowing us to come to this alien, cold country ... I think I didn't write to me mother for about two months. But of course it wasn't her fault because there was an economic blockade around the country ... We used to buy flour at home by the sackful for 8s and overnight it went up to £2 2s. You couldn't buy anything and you couldn't sell anything. Shopkeepers were going bankrupt with this economic blockade ... because in them days Britain was all-powerful wasn't it? And how dare little Ireland get out from Mother England? We were all being punished – that is the real reason why there was such an exodus.
> (Joan, b. 1915, Co. Mayo)

Joan's sentiments, which were similar to those of several other respondents, can be explained by the cultural climate which permeated Ireland during the years when most of the women left. In the first forty years after partition, the new Irish state pursued successive policies which emphasised not only its political but also its economic, spiritual and cultural independence from its colonial past. Gaelic sports, music and language and the Catholic faith were vigorously promoted. Attempts at economic self-sufficiency during this period can be seen as another example of the Irish state ideologically distancing itself from Britain which was by far its main trading partner. Southern Ireland could not win its economic war with industrialised Britain but material deficits were translated as spiritual superiority. De Valera's famous St Patrick's Day broadcast of 1943 epitomizes an idealized rural Ireland which dominated official rhetoric and ignored the reality of economic stagnation and high emigration:

> That Ireland which we dreamed of would be the home of a people who valued material wealth only as a basis of right living, of a people who

were satisfied with frugal comfort and devoted their leisure to things of
the spirit; a land whose countryside would be bright with cosy home-
steads, whose fields and villages would be joyous with sounds of industry,
the romping of sturdy children, the contests of athletic youths, the
laughter of comely maidens; whose firesides would be the forums of
the wisdom of serene old age.[26]

Poverty, euphemistically disguised as 'frugal comfort' by de Valera,
forced thousands of Irish 'athletic youths' and 'comely maidens' to
emigrate and those who went to England had the added burden of
the negative preconceptions of that country which they had grown
up with. One emigrant woman saw the absurdity of this idealisation
of rural Ireland, combined with anti-English rhetoric, when the mass
exportation of people across the Irish Sea was continuing. Maura,
like Joan, was another eighteen year old emigrant. She left Roscommon for Lancashire in 1945 because she could not find paid work at
home but she blamed the Irish government for having to leave, and
for making her psychologically ill-equipped for the move:

> They taught us to hate England and then they sent us here! (Maura,
> b. 1927, Co. Roscommon)

It is ironic, that it was during this period of post-independence,
when official rhetoric was promoting all things Irish and denigrating
all things British, that Britain replaced the United States as the main
destination of Irish emigrants in 1929.[27]

In the analysis of the life-histories of the women who had mainly
economic reasons for emigrating an important theme emerged. It
was not a desire to financially improve their own circumstances but
to assist their families which was the most common motivation of
emigrants. The economic situation of her family and her order in
the family were important factors in determining if, and also how
soon, a woman emigrated. The remittances sent by older siblings
were often needed to maintain the family at home and they were
sometimes used to pay for the secondary education of younger
children in the family:

> All the children who went in the '40s and '50's did the same thing. We
> went to help the younger children, and to educate them. (Lena, b. 1930,
> Co. Galway)

Several respondents noted that their younger brothers or sisters
progressed to secondary education whereas they and their older
siblings did not. Most of the respondents only attended national
schools and left when they were about fourteen; a lesser number
went on to technical schools, run by nuns; and one woman, Maeve,

attended private convent boarding schools and graduated from Dublin University with a degree in medicine. The reason why most of the respondents left the Irish state education system at fourteen was the same as it was for most children, in Britain as well as Ireland, at that time; their parents could not afford to keep them at school. Education beyond the standard state primary (national school) level had to be paid for and state provision for bright but poor pupils was scant in Ireland: in the inter-war years only 2–4% of secondary school entrants received scholarships from public funds and as late as 1960–61 only about 600 public secondary scholarships were awarded when between 70–80,000 pupils a year were finishing their primary education.[28] Only 214 means-tested local authority scholarships for university education were provided as late as 1962/63.[29] One respondent also received a secondary education because of financial help from an emigrant relative. Annie, who kept house for two bachelor farmers in Cavan when she was fourteen, was enabled to leave this job after ten months because her aunt offered to pay for her to go to a technical school:

> I had an aunt who came home from America, and that helped me to sort it out and I got back to school. She said to me mother: "I'm amazed at you having a girl of fourteen out working like that!" ... I decided I would leave, when I got this opportunity to go to the technical school. That really was your passport to life – getting to the technical school. I was so thrilled and so delighted. (Annie, b. 1929, Co. Cavan)

Some women had other than economic reasons to leave Ireland. One such reason was to conceal a pregnancy if the woman was unmarried. Irish attitudes to sex and sexuality are investigated later in the book and it will suffice to say here that unmarried mothers were not generally tolerated in Irish society at this time and the pregnancy of a single woman was usually regarded as bringing shame upon her whole family. Some women emigrated alone and hid their pregnancy from their family in Ireland but there is also a pattern of female family members colluding to arrange emigrations in order to conceal unmarried pregnancies. Siobhan recalled that an unmarried, pregnant sister of her husband's went to stay with her married sister in Scotland and their mother went over from Donegal for the birth. This had occurred before Siobhan's marriage and her husband, the eldest child of the family, was left to care for the younger children in his widowed mother's absence:

> His mother went over to Scotland and left him looking after the younger ones at home. She'd gone over because that one was having a baby in Scotland and she was staying wi' another married sister. She had the

baby adopted. But me husband didn't know, his mother didn't tell him. They sorta kept things from the boy. He didn't know until he came over here and I told him. (Siobhan, b. 1938, Co. Donegal)

This pattern of female family members collectively arranging the emigration of pregnant women is evident in several of the life histories. Lily had been living in Morecambe for two years when her mother asked her to arrange the marriage of her pregnant sister. She also provided a home for the young family until they could return to Ireland. Her testimony is interesting because it illustrates that Protestants [Lily and her family were Baptists] were as keen to hide family indiscretions from their neighbours in Ireland as Catholics were:

> My mother wrote to me and she said: "I'm sending her over, arrange a wedding!" It was a bit of a rush wedding. They came over here because it might not have been the right thing for people to know at home ... The child was born here but they didn't like it here and they went home. They didn't go back to Athlone ... they got a job outside Wicklow (Lily, b. 1929, Athlone)

The young couple had not wanted to emigrate, or even leave Athlone, but they did so in order to protect the reputations of their families. The circumstances of Lily's own emigration in 1950 also highlight how emigration was often undertaken less for individual than for family needs. Lily had a good job in a shop and she was very happy living in Athlone. In her life history she revealed that neither she nor her sisters were allowed to date Catholic boys when they were young but there were comparatively few Protestants in the town and her family were related to a lot of them. She had no intention of emigrating but was forced to do so by her mother when she became friendly with a male cousin. Her mother also wanted Lily to move near to two of her uncles who had lost contact with the family in Athlone:

> I was friendly with a cousin at home. I used to go to his house a lot and we became very friendly. I didn't think there was anything wrong with it but quite suddenly I was told: "You're not to go over there anymore." I think my mother saw what was coming and decided it was time I was shipped out. She had two reasons, that was one, and the other one was to find out what her brothers were doing ... I had no notion of emigrating and I had no inclination to be a nurse. But my mother wrote off to the Lancaster Infirmary and I was taken on as a student nurse ... In those days you had to be obedient to what your parents said ... I remember thinking: "I don't really want to be a nurse. I don't really want to be going anywhere" (Lily, b. 1929, Athlone)

Lily hated nursing and soon after emigrating she left Lancaster Infirmary and moved into her uncle's home in nearby Morecambe where she found work as a shop assistant, a job she had enjoyed in Athlone before she was forced to leave. Claire was another woman who did not want to emigrate but her mother decided otherwise. She was eighteen and had been working for two years in Northern Ireland when, on a visit home, her mother decided that she should go to live with an aunt in Halifax. Similar to Lily's situation, it was because her mother wanted her to end a romantic relationship:

> I went home to Clare and my mother didn't want me to go back to Northern Ireland again ... I met a young boy there and he was a non-Catholic, and o'course they were all against it in those days. She wouldn't let me back. So she says: "You can go to Halifax in Yorkshire and you can stay there." So I went to my auntie's. (Claire, b. 1932, Co. Clare)

Not only could family pressures push emigrants out of Ireland, they could also draw them abroad. Sheila was born in Dublin in 1923 and she spent most of her life caring for relatives in Ireland and England. At the age of nineteen she left her job in a Dublin mill to nurse her dying mother. She then took care of her younger brothers and sisters for five years whilst her father was working in England. When her father returned home she was persuaded, against her wishes, to look after her uncle's family in Lancaster:

> I came to Liverpool in 1947, then I came here to Lancaster. Me uncle was desperate, his wife was dying and there were four small children. I started the whole routine all over again. I nursed me mother until she died and I nursed his wife until she died ... He was away in the Merchant Navy so I looked after his wife and then I had those children to look after. I wasn't going to do it at first because I thought well I'd done it once, me brothers and sisters like, you know, and it was a hard job ... I didn't really know what to do, you know, but I did feel sorry for him. (Sheila, b. 1923, Dublin)

Sheila lived in her uncle's house in Lancaster for over thirty years, caring for his children into adulthood and nursing him when he became infirm.

The overwhelming impression gained from the oral life histories is that whether the basic cause of each woman's emigration was for economic (which were the majority), or for social reasons, it was most often undertaken in order to fulfil family rather than individual needs. The strength of the women's loyalty to their families can be explained by the enduring dominance of the family in the ideology of Irish society. The symbol of the family was closely linked to the rural ideal which was illustrated earlier in the chapter. Ciaran

McCullagh has located the roots of the Irish ideology of the family in the post-Famine period [30] and it had lost none of its symbolic force by the 20th century. Article 41 of the 1937 Constitution recognised the family to be 'the natural primary and fundamental unit group of society' and placed the ideal role of women in the home, caring for the family: 'the State recognises that by her life within the home, woman gives to the State a support without which the common good cannot be achieved'.[31] It is ironic that during this period, when Irish women's roles were becoming increasingly defined by familial duties within the home, hundreds of thousands of Irish women were leaving their family homes and emigrating. Between 1926 and 1951 about 52,000 women left Southern Ireland for the United States and 180,000 went to Britain.[32]

When the means by which the women left Ireland are analysed, family involvement is also found to be an important feature of the process. Only three women arranged and experienced their emigration without the involvement of family members. Most women either left for destinations where they already had relatives, or they were accompanied by relatives. The three married emigrant women all accompanied their husbands to towns where the husband had secured a job.

Several of the respondents left Ireland to train as nurses in England and it was common for them to either go with a sister or a cousin, or to go to a hospital where a relative was already working. When Theresa left Co. Roscommon in 1948 she followed this common pattern of training at the hospital where her sister was a nurse:

> After the War they were very scarce of nurses over here and my eldest sister went ... She was over here a year and then she came home on holiday and she wanted to bring me back with her. So the same hospital took the two of us ... She only wanted me to come with her for the company, you know, because we were always together at home. (Theresa, b. 1928, Co. Roscommon)

Theresa only went to nurse in Southport because her sister wanted her company. Agnes herself decided that she wanted to leave Roscommon to train as a nurse in Rochdale but her mother would not let her come to England alone and made her reluctant sister go with her in 1945:

> The War was on and my mother was very much against us going to England ... I had applied to this hospital, Birch Hill in Rochdale, Lancashire and got accepted. But me mother was determined that we both should go. I don't really know did my sister want to go that much: she kinda drifted into it because I was going. (Agnes, b. 1925, Coventry)

The previous two quotes are illustrative not only of the trend for women to emigrate with, or to the same place as, their sisters; they also demonstrate once again how women sometimes drifted into emigration to please other family members.

Even entering the Church was not always a solitary move for women. There is also a pattern of women leaving Ireland to join religious orders with female family members. When Sr Kevin left Ireland to become a novice nun in 1945, she did not go alone:

> I entered just after the War with my three cousins. (Sr Kevin, b. Co. Kerry, 1924)

Sr Kevin and her cousins decided to join the Ursulines after the order had held a recruitment drive in their local parish in Co. Kerry. Another respondent, Maggie, left factory work in Derry and volunteered to join an order of missionaries. After two years as a novice nun in Lousiana, however, she left the order. Her recollections show how friends (or in Sr Kevin's case, family) often joined the same religious orders after attending religious events designed to recruit people into the Church:

> The Missionaries always came round, ye know, doing Retreats. And o'course they were looking for somebody to go to the Mission fields. There was quite a few from around our way in fact. There's Kathleen Tolan, she's a Reverend Mother out in Africa. We were all friends that went round together. Rosaleen McGee, she died in Africa. May Devaney, she's a Sister in London. Oh they always had a good response when they done the Retreats in Derry. (Maggie, b. 1926, Co. Donegal)

These examples suggest that Catholic Church recruitment practices encouraged women to join the Church alongside family members and friends.

It has been shown here that the families of female emigrants were often crucially involved in both the reasons why, and the ways in which, the women emigrated. The next section will investigate the reasons why Irish women settled in Lancashire.

Why did Irish women go to Lancashire?

Even though they settled in Lancashire, it was not always the destination which emigrants had intended or preferred to go to when they left Ireland. Emigration to Britain was seen as an inferior alternative to emigration to America by some of the older respondents. Before the United States placed quota restrictions on immigrants in the 1920s it was the most common destination of Irish emigrants and most of the respondents had relatives living there:

> Emigration was completely stopped to America because of the Wall St.
> Crash. And that's where we all would have gone because all my father's
> people were in the U.S. Oh yes, we'd have all gone. Well five of me sisters
> went when they could, you know. (Joan, b. 1915, Co. Mayo)

Intending emigrants had to pass a medical examination before they
could leave for the United States and this held a certain prestige for
many people. Emigration to Britain was, however, stigmatised for
the very same reason:

> Everybody in our village, that went anywhere, went to America. But
> you had to pass a medical exam, and only those that failed the medical
> exam came to England. That's the truth. You knew when you seen
> somebody going to England that they'd failed the medical exam.
> (Philomena, b. 1917, Co. Mayo)

For two of the women, America was their initial emigrant destination. Attracta went to live near her brother in Chicago in 1933 and
Maggie went as a novice nun to Baton Rouge, Louisiana, in 1950.

There is a general stereotype of Irish emigrants leaving small
farming communities and heading straight for large British cities,
where they are ill-equipped to cope with urban living:

> The background from which the Irish immigrant to Great Britain has
> come has, in the main, been a rural one. This background has done little
> to prepare the immigrant for urban life in Britain.[33]

At first glance, the oral history respondents would appear to fit this
stereotype since 77% of them were born in rural areas of Ireland
and all of them settled in urban areas of Lancashire. However, the
briefly mentioned fact that two of the respondents also lived in the
United States indicates that the stereotype is too simple. Qualitative
evidence from the oral life-histories employed here can provide
details which are not apparent in quantitative sources like the census
of population which can show how many people left a certain place,
or how many were living in another, but give no indication of the
migration of individuals over a period of time. The migration patterns of the women in this sample up to the mid-1960s show that
although most of the respondents were born in rural areas, many
of them had experience of living in towns before they moved to
Lancashire, or even England.[34] Molly, for example, grew up in rural
Co. Longford but she had lived in Dublin for three years before she
emigrated to Lancaster in 1951 and she recalled that her time in
Dublin prepared her for emigration:

> I was in Dublin for a bit. It sort of broke me in because if I'd come from
> the middle of Ireland over here I would have found it a lot different.

We weren't backward but the Dublin people would think you were –
coming from the country. They'd think you knew nothing – that was
Dublin. I lived in Dublin for three years, so I was sort of used to people
and things going on around me. I didn't find it as strange as if I'd come
right from the middle of Ireland over here. That helped me a bit. (Molly,
b. 1931, Co. Longford)

J. A. Jackson's previously cited stereotype of Irish emigrants coming to Britain prior to the 1960s having little or no experience of
urban living has been shown to be false. Although most Irish
emigrants were born in rural areas and the Irish lived mainly in the
towns and cities of Britain, it should not be presumed that they had
not lived and worked in towns before coming to Britain. The
evidence here suggests that they most probably had.

Having established that Lancashire was not always the first choice
of destination for the respondents, nor was it always their first place
of residence after emigration, the women's reasons for settling in
Lancashire will now be assessed. Whether they had emigrated for
social or economic reasons, by far the most common reason why
the women in this study moved to Lancashire was that they already
had relatives living in the county:

I came over to nurse at the Lancaster Infirmary … My sister was here
and I came over to my sister. (Molly, b. 1931, Co. Longford)

I came to my cousin's in Manchester. And then she moved to Blackpool
so I went there. (Bernadette, b. 1915, Co. Mayo)

It was not only to female relations that the women went. They
also went to live in the same towns, and often in the same houses,
as male relatives. Previous quotes from Lily and Sheila showed that
they lived with their respective uncles in Morecambe and Lancaster.
Attracta also moved from London to Morecambe in 1940 and lived
in the same lodging house as one of her brothers. There is also
much evidence from the oral life-histories that Irish emigrants
moved to areas other than Lancashire because they had relatives
living there:

When I left Ireland I'd already got two sisters living in Warwickshire.
One of them was married and I went to live with her in Warwick. (Elsie,
b. 1931, Co. Wexford)

I had four sisters went to San Francisco … One went to America when
she was only seventeen, and then the other three went out after. They
went out to her. (Maura, b. 1927, Co. Roscommon)

Irish men also moved to towns where they had relatives. Rosie left

Dublin, with her husband and baby daughter in 1952, to settle in Lancaster because he had a sister already living in the town:

> James was out of work and couldn't get a job, you know … His sister lived here in Lancaster and she asked us to come over and offered to put us up. (Rosie, b. 1926, Dublin)

Several of the respondents also provided accommodation for emigrant relatives once they had settled in Lancashire. Two of Annie's sisters emigrated and moved in with Annie and her husband and young family in St Helen's in the 1950s. The arrangement was as beneficial to Annie as it was to her sisters, since they paid her for lodging there and one sister looked after the children, enabling Annie to return to nursing:

> One o' my sisters came over in 1955. She came to do nursing and she stayed with me. Then the year after that, my other sister came and she stayed with me. She worked in a factory … They were both working so, obviously, they gave me something towards their keep and that really helped when you had small children … One sister, Eileen, had an ulcer then and she wasn't that well to work in the factory … So she housekept for me and I went into nursing again. (Annie, b. 1929, Co. Cavan)

Family emigration networks were extensive amongst the respondents to this study. Irish immigrants, not just in Lancashire, but in other areas of Britain and the U.S.A., often lived in particular towns mainly because they already had relatives living there.

An important finding of this chapter is that the stereotype of most Irish immigrants in Britain having a background of little or no experience of urban living is flawed. This stereotype is based on a quantitative analysis of the numbers of Irish people who left certain areas of Ireland, and the numbers who settled in particular British locations, at certain times. It does not show the full picture because it contains the inherent presumption that emigrants simply left one place for another without revealing the places which they might also have lived in between the two. The depth of information provided in emigrants' life-histories provides a source for detailing individual migration patterns and the patterns provided in this chapter show that although 77% of the emigrants were born in rural Ireland and all of them lived in towns after they moved to Lancashire, most of the women had experienced urban living before they had moved to the county, or before emigrating to Britain.

The main theme running through this chapter, however, is that of extensive family involvement in Irish emigration. Women left Southern Ireland because of various economic or social reasons but, whatever the basic cause was, it was usually concerning the emigrant's family as much as herself individually. Emigration was most often undertaken in order to fulfil the needs or expectations of the emigrant's family. Evidence has also been shown of family pressures pushing women out of Ireland, or drawing them to England, against their own wishes. No resistance to this pressure has been shown from the women in this sample. Existing family networks were also the main reasons for emigrant women locating in particular areas. Only in the area of concealing a pregnancy was the network gendered. In other instances, women were as likely to stay with male relatives as female and vice versa.

Explaining the high rate of female emigration to Britain in the 1940s and '50s, Ide O'Carroll has suggested that: 'Essential to this move was the desire to distance themselves from control by family and patriarchal society.'[35] Whilst Irish society has been shown to be patriarchal and family-oriented, as demonstrated by the strength of, and women's position as dutiful carer in, the ideology of the family, the findings of this chapter contradict O'Carroll's view. Family influence, if not always control, was evident throughout the female emigration process; from the decision to leave to the choice of destination. Ironically, for many women leaving home was often the only way to ensure the economic survival, or the good name, of the family. An investigation of emigrant women's contact with their family homes in Ireland in the next chapter will discover whether these family ties were stretched or severed by emigration.

Notes

1. See appendix, table 1: Population of Ireland, 1841–1961.
2. Rita M. Rhodes, *Women and the family in post-Famine Ireland*, 1992, p. 243.
3. J. H. Johnson, 'The distribution of Irish emigration', *Irish Geography*, 21, 1988, pp. 78–87.
4. R. F. Foster, *Modern Ireland*, 1989, pp. 352–355.
5. Liam Kennedy, *The Modern Industrialization of Ireland*, 1989, p. 4.
6. Bronwen Walter, in P. King (ed.), *Contemporary Irish Migration*, 1991, p. 11.
7. W. E. Vaughan & A. J. Fitzpatrick (eds), *Irish Historical Statistics*, 1978, p. 266.
8. J. J. Lee, *Ireland 1912–1985*, p. 379, whose source was: F. Tobin, *The best of decades*, 1984, p. 156.
9. P. J. Drudy, *Ireland and Britain since 1922*, 1986, pp. 108–10.
10. See appendix, table 2: Birthplace of respondents.
11. Rita M. Rhodes, *Women and the Family in Post-Famine Ireland*, 1992, pp. 248–249.

12. See appendix, table 3: Average annual net emigration from Southern Ireland classified by gender, 1871–1971.
13. Robert E. Kennedy, *The Irish*, 1973, p. 74; J. A. Jackson, *The Irish in Britain*, 1963, pp. 104–106.
14. See appendix, table 4: Year of emigration of respondents.
15. *Commission on Emigration and other Population Problems*, 1956, p. 129.
16. Pauric Travers, in Patrick O'Sullivan (ed.), *The Irish World Wide, Vol. 4, Irish Women*, pp. 148–149; and also in O'Dowd & Wichert (eds), *Chattel, Servant or Citizen*, 1995, p. 189.
17. See appendix, table 5: Age of respondents on initial emigration from Ireland. Although the total number of respondents to the oral history sample is 40, Maureen is not included in this table since she did not emigrate from Ireland. The 81% is, therefore, calculated from 34 out of a total of 39.
18. P. J. Drudy, 'Migration between Ireland and Britain since Independence', *Irish Studies* 5, 1986, pp. 112–114.
19. Frank Neal, *North West Labour History*, no. 16, 1991/92, p. 15.
20. Colin Pooley, in R. Swift and S. Gilley, *The Irish in Britain*, p. 66.
21. Bradley Snell, 'Geographical distribution of the Irish-born population in England 1961', unpublished M.A. thesis, Lancaster University, 1996.
22. Robert E. Kennedy Jr, *The Irish*, 1973, p. 2.
23. Census of Population, Ireland, 1961.
24. J. A. Jackson, *The Irish in Britain*, 1963, p. 27.
25. Tom Inglis, *Moral Monopoly*, 1987, pp. 12–13; Sean Glynn, *I.E.S.H.*, VIII, 1981, p. 52; Robert E. Kennedy, *The Irish*, 1973, pp. 110–138.
26. Irish Press, 18th March, 1943, p. 1. Reproduced in Terence Brown, *Ireland: A Social and Cultural History*, 1985, p. 146.
27. P. J. Drudy, 'Migration between Ireland and Britain since Independence', *Irish Studies* 5, 1986, pp. 107–123.
28. J. J. Lee, *Ireland 1912–1985: Politics and Society*, 1989, p. 132.
29. John Coolahan, *Irish Education*, 1981, p. 78.
30. Ciaran McCullagh, 'A Tie That Blinds: Family and Ideology in Ireland', *The Economic and Social Review*, 1991, pp. 199–211.
31. *Bunreacht na h'Eireann* (Constitution of Ireland), 1937.
32. Pauric Travers, 'Emigration and Gender: The Case of Ireland, 1922–60', in Mary O'Dowd and Sabine Wichert (eds), *Chattel, Servant or Citizen*, 1995, p. 190.
33. J. A. Jackson, *The Irish in Britain*, 1963, p. 81.
34. See appendix, table 6: Migration patterns of respondents.
35. Ide O'Carroll, *Models for Movers*, 1990, p. 12.

Home away from home

5. *Above*: Farmhouse, Co. Sligo, 1929. Single-storey cottages were the most common form of housing in rural Ireland. Reproduced courtesy of Colm Mulligan.

6. *Right*: Spring Garden Street, Lancaster, 1927. The tall, narrow terraced houses of working-class Lancashire streets were a stark contrast to the low-level cottages of rural Ireland. Reproduced courtesy of Lancaster City Museums.

Working Lives

Naas.   zl

Wanted immediately for all parts of England. Cooks, cook-generals, mothers' helps, etc, trained and un-trained, for private houses, colleges and hotels. Top wages. Fares paid. Write us with confidence enclosing references. We have a job to suit you. — Town and County Catholic Employment · Agency, 85 Middle Abbey Street, Dublin.   3097a3feb4 Wanted, cook-general, indoor or out-

7. In the 1950s, advertisements recruiting women for work in England were a common sight in Irish newspapers. This one is from The Leinster Leader, Saturday, January 22, 1955. Reproduced courtesy of Kildare County Library.

8. The late Mary Gilligan proudly posing in her uniform after becoming a nurse at the Northern Hospital, Cheetham Hill in 1937. Reproduced courtesy of Irish Community Care, Manchester.

9. Many of the nurses graduating here in 1963 were Irish, including Nula Bradwell (nee Kerins) who went on to work in Crumpsall Hosptial for 33 years. Reproduced courtesy of Nula Bradwell and Irish Community Care, Manchester.

10. The Reilly sisters from Co. Cavan enjoying a day off in Blackpool where they worked in domestic service in the 1940s.

11. The AEI factory, Trafford Park, Manchester, employed many Irish women. This picture shows women at work in the packing department. Reproduced courtesy of Irish Community Care, Manchester.

12. Women from the packing line of Kellogs, Trafford Park, Manchester. Nora Higgins, a Roscommon woman, remembered working with many other Irish women during her 22 years at Kellogs. Reproduced courtesy of Irish Community Care, Manchester.

CHAPTER THREE

Keeping in touch

In the previous chapter, an important theme of the book emerged: that of the influence of the family on Irish women's lives. For many women, family influence and involvement was evident in the reasons why, and the ways in which, they emigrated. The purpose of this chapter is to assess the extent to which Irish women either maintained or rejected family ties after emigration. Oral life histories provide an ideal source for discovering the various ways in which Irish women in Britain and their families in Ireland kept in touch with each other; and also the ways in which they avoided contact. In her oral history of Irish women in America from the 1920s to the 1980s, Ide O'Carroll argued that female emigrants rejected Irish society and 'turned their backs on Ireland'. Furthermore, 'the rejection of family life was a major theme in the story of Irish women emigrants to the U.S.A.'.[1] In light of the main conclusion of chapter 3, that family influence was apparent in most aspects of the female emigration process, O'Carroll's findings will again be questioned in this chapter.

Contact with home and family after emigration

Telephones were not generally accessible to working-class people in Ireland or England during the period of this study and letters remained the cheapest and most utilized form of communication between the two countries. The respondents regularly wrote to, and received letters back from, their families in Ireland, apart from during the Second World War when some mail was restricted for security reasons. The nature of the letters which passed between women and their relatives in Ireland shows a pattern of transmitting only good news wherever possible:

> Oh you always wrote, always. But you never told the bad things. No, nobody ever does; you just told the good things ... It didn't matter how bad you were, you'd suffer in silence, you'd pretend everything was splendid. (Joan, b. 1915, Co. Mayo)

It was not only emigrants who portrayed a positive image of their lives in their letters home, their families in Ireland did the same:

> Me mother would write great big long letters. And she'd tell you about

everybody you knew; where they were; if they were home; the children that were born. She'd tell you about the animals and all the news from there. That was your lifeline. She didn't tell us anything bad. Yet there must've been bad things mustn't there? But she never did tell us them. (Philomena, b. 1917, Co. Mayo)

Emigrants could also prioritise news which they knew their families would want to hear. When Agnes came to Rochdale, to train as a nurse in 1945, she was delighted to be able to inform her mother in Roscommon that she was keeping up her religious practices:

My mother had a awful thing about being allowed to practise your religious duties and we were always called on Holydays of Obligation for Mass. We were on the wards at half-seven so the Mass was usually at half-six and we were called for it. I was very glad to be able to devote one page of a letter to tell my mother that we were called for Mass. (Agnes, b. 1925, Coventry)

It was easier to include reassuring information than to exclude news which would alarm the family at home but one emigrant managed to conceal her life-threatening illness from her parents despite writing to them regularly during her six-month stay in an isolation hospital in 1940. She was only able to conceal this information with the agreement of her brothers and sisters in England:

I was six months on my back in the isolation hospital and it was touch and go because diphtheria affects your heart. I was so weak. And I kept writing home, just three lines, and the ward sister would post it for me. But I never told them that I was in hospital. I told my family not to tell my mother and father. (Attracta, b. 1915, Co. Sligo)

Written contact was not only selective but it could also be fabricated. Emigrant letters were a source not just of news but entertainment for the family in Ireland, and they could be embroidered accordingly:

I was always writing letters to my mother and I was always writing things that made her laugh. Long rubbishy letters, you know, telling her about the mental hospital patients. Most of it was made up but it was just to give her a laugh, you know. (Lena, b. 1930, Co. Galway)

It appears that when both parents were still living it was the mother who most usually corresponded with emigrant daughters:

I wrote, yeah. Me mother obviously wrote back, you know. One's father doesn't write really. The mother does all the writing – it's left to the mother. (Annie, b. 1929, Co. Cavan)

13. Home for the holidays. Women and children on the beach at Duncannon, Co. Wexford in the early 1960s. Reproduced courtesy of Mary Walsh.

The respondents generally reported that they enjoyed receiving letters containing news from home and claimed to have kept in regular contact by mail with their families, not just in Ireland but throughout the world, before the telephone became widely available and largely replaced the emigrant letter. The oral evidence shows that the contents of emigrants' letters should not necessarily be accepted as a complete, or even accurate, representation of the everyday life of emigrants and their families in Ireland. An over-positive image was often portrayed in letters from both sides of the Irish Sea. Female emigrants said that they consciously cultivated an optimistic view of their lives abroad partly for their own self-esteem and also to alleviate their parents' anxiety; and parents probably did as much for the same reasons. This has implications for research based on emigrants' letters but, for the purposes of this study, the fact that emigrants and their family (usually mothers) in Ireland were keen to send reassuring messages that things were going well for them suggests that they had generally affectionate family relationships.

Letters were not the only form of postal communication between emigrants and their families in Ireland. By the middle of the twentieth century the sending of parcels and money was a well-established tradition amongst Irish emigrants and the importance of emigrants' remittances to the Irish economy was noted by the *Commission on Emigration and other Population Problems*, which conducted a major survey between 1948 and 1954 and published its results in 1956:

> Many of the families of those who emigrated have had their incomes increased by emigrants' remittances. In some cases, this increase in income has made it unnecessary for other members of the family to emigrate, but, in other cases, it has been the means of enabling them to do so. Emigrants' remittances are an important item in the national economy: they partly redress the adverse balance of trade, they may stimulate production, or in certain circumstances they may have a limited inflationary effect. Their social effect is to bring about greater equality in the distribution of wealth.[2]

Many Irish families relied on money and parcels sent from their offspring abroad and Maura's experience was typical of many

14. The mail boat 'Scotia' about to leave Holyhead for Ireland, 1937. Reproduced courtesy of Father Browne S. J. Collection.

emigrant women's. She worked as a chambermaid in Morecambe and before she married she sent most of her wages back to her family in Roscommon:

> My generation was great for sending money. I used to send as much as ever I could. You'd send and do without, you know. I sent it to my mother. They needed it really because there was four younger than me still at home. Everybody that went sent it. I remember a woman in Ireland and if her daughters wrote and they hadn't sent money she usen't to answer it! She wouldn't answer it unless there was money in it. You could send it by telegram and they used to be waiting for the telegrams in Ireland. (Maura, b. 1927, Co. Roscommon)

Maura's recollections show not only that the sending of money home was widespread amongst Irish emigrants, but also that there was a difference in attitudes to the practice amongst families. Maura recalled later in her interview that her parents were grateful for the money which she sent and within the quote she expressed no resentment at leaving herself short since her family needed the money more than she did. The woman whom she remembered in Ireland,

15. Passengers aboard the mail boat 'Scotia', 1937. Reproduced courtesy of Father Browne S. J. Collection.

however, expected her daughters to send money every time they wrote to her and ungraciously ignored them when they did not do so. The conclusion drawn from all the respondents' testimonies is that, although a few did, emigrants generally did not resent sending money home, since they appreciated how much it was needed, and parents were usually grateful.

The most usual impression of the Irish emigration experience is one of families being poorer in Ireland than their more affluent emigrant members abroad, but this was not always the case. Molly's family background in Co. Longford was not prosperous, she was one of thirteen children born to a gamekeeper and his wife, but when she was struggling to raise her own six children in Lancaster her mother sent parcels from Ireland:

> Every Christmas, for years and years, I never had to buy anything for Christmas because about a week before every Christmas she sent me a parcel. And there was a turkey, there was butter and there was sauce. There was everything that you could think of, pudding and everything, for Christmas. I never used to have to buy anything. She was so good to me. Always at Christmas I used to wait for this box coming. (Molly, b. 1931, Co. Longford)

Most respondents reported sending money or parcels to their families in Ireland, at least while they were single, but some women never sent any and others received gifts from Ireland. Although it is impossible to quantify the extent of remittances which were sent from both sides of the Irish sea, the overall impression is that it was more normal for emigrants to offer financial support to their families at home; but there were exceptions to this rule and some families in Ireland assisted their children abroad. The transfer of gifts and money across the Irish Sea appears to have been extensive.

The greater proximity of Britain than the previously favoured emigrant destination of the U.S.A., and improved and cheaper sea passage across the Irish Sea, made visits home more accessible to Irish emigrants in the mid-twentieth century than at any previous time. Irish women in Lancashire were favourably placed on the west coast with the two ports of Heysham and Liverpool offering regular sailings to Ireland. Apart from proximity and affordabilty, social factors also determined whether or not women visited their families in Ireland. It has already been shown that some women were selective in what they wrote to their families and the fear of disclosing a secret also kept some woman from travelling home. Attracta, who omitted to inform her parents that she had contracted diphtheria, did not visit them for two years until the signs of her illness were no longer visible. One respondent, Bernadette, gave birth to an illegitimate son a few years after emigrating to Lancashire. She wrote and told her parents in Co. Mayo of his existence when he was eight months old and they proved supportive, but she did not go home when he was a child for fear of embarrassing the family. Ireland was, however, the usual – most often the only – holiday destination of the women interviewed and most respondents spoke of 'going home' as often as they could afford to. Single working women, especially nurses who did not have to take fixed holidays, were often able to accrue their leave entitlements and have extended summer holidays in Ireland. The arrival of emigrants home on holiday was cause for celebration in rural Ireland and Kathleen and her sisters timed their holidays for the season following harvesting, when more of their family and neighbours would be free to socialise:

> I used to go home. Every year I went home for a month's holiday while me mother was alive, you know. I went home every September. We used to have a good time. All the work was nearly done then, the harvest was saved and everything, and people had time to come visiting. We used to go from house to house. You'd be invited from one house to another, you know, and they'd have a dance for you that night. We used to get an accordion player, or a fiddle player or something, and the crowd used to come. We were dancing till 6 o'clock in the morning in the country houses; it was lovely. There was one time – me sisters and I used to go home for a month, you know – and the week before we come back we had one and a half hours sleep only! We come back, and I got in – I was living in the nurses home at the time. I arrived back on the Sunday morning about 8 o'clock, and Mass used to be a quarter past nine at the hospital, and I was so tired I laid on the bed and I never knew a thing till Monday dinnertime! We had one and a half hours sleep, that's all; on the boat coming over. We had such a good time; we danced and danced and danced, we danced ourselves silly. But I had to go in front of Matron the following day because I didn't turn up for duty on Monday morning. (Kathleen, b. 1921, Co. Leitrim)

There was a labour shortage in post-war Britain and when the National Health Service was founded in 1948 some health authorities used subsidised travel home as an incentive to recruit Irish women into nursing:

> I came to Manchester and for the three years I was training our fare was paid back every six months. It was subsidised under some scheme through the Labour Exchange. I think I had to pay something like 7/6d. But the English girls, which I can understand, were furious about it because they couldn't afford their fares home on the buses and our fares were being paid to go back to Ireland … So I went back on the subsidised trips

every six months. Back home they'd be waiting all the time for good news, and they got good news. (Aine, b. 1929, Co. Cavan)

Factory workers were usually more restricted than nurses were, in taking their holidays when they pleased, but two Irish women in Manchester regularly took longer than their official leave allocation and their employer made allowances for them:

> From when we went to England me sister and I always went home twice a year at August and Christmas. We worked in a shirt factory in Manchester and Mr Bernstein, our Jewish boss, he used to always call it the "Irish month" because we'd go for a month and we'd stop six weeks! That went on right up till we got married. (Patricia, b. 1925, Co. Donegal)

Having children, rather than getting married, was the point in women's life-cycles which most affected their ability to visit Ireland. The expense of taking the whole family over appears to be the main reason why some Irish women went home less often after they became mothers:

> When the children was little we didn't go home every year; about every two years, or every three years sometimes. It was as often as I could afford, otherwise I would ha' been there every year. (Siobhan, b. 1938, Co. Donegal)

Noreen was married to a labourer, who like her came from Donegal, and she struggled but just managed to afford the trips home for themselves and their seven children:

> We used to go home nearly every year, for a week or a fortnight. It was hard. 'Cause it was hard to keep the children clothed never mind anything else! But I worked nearly all me life while I was here. Ye had tae work in with them [the children] as best you could. I done mostly nights 'cause me husband was at home then. (Noreen, b. 1913, Co. Donegal)

Women in better-off circumstances could spend whole summers in Ireland with their children. Their husbands often stayed working in England for part of this time and joined them later:

> Me sister and myself went over to Ireland for the whole summer. The men stopped in Manchester and worked. He would come over for the last two weeks then … It was lovely for the children to have a good holiday over there and the free life that they had. Me brother and me sister's children and mine they used to be fishing up the rivers catching trout. And making their own fishing rods with the long salley rod with the leaf on the end and the fly. (Patricia, b. 1925, Co. Donegal)

Patricia, who provided the last quote, viewed her children's summers

in Ireland as preferable to spending them in urban Manchester.
Maeve could also afford to bring her children to Ireland for the
whole summer as she and her husband were both doctors in Liverpool. She shared the Irish nationalist sympathies of her family but
was sensitive to the fact that her children were born in middle-class
England and wanted them to spend time in Ireland in order to make
their own informed decisions as to which culture they identified
with:

> We'd split our holidays and he'd take them for a month and then he'd
> come back and I'd go for the next month … So they grew up knowing
> Irish people and knowing the culture of Ireland you see. (Maeve, b. 1917,
> Co. Tipperary)

Maeve's three children subsequently adopted Irish identities; her
two sons chose to attend Irish universities and one son and a
daughter now live and work in the west of Ireland. A desire to
acquaint their children with their relations in Ireland and their Irish
cultural inheritance was often expressed by mothers, but ironically
some could not afford to travel to Ireland as much after they had
children.

Women also made visits to Ireland for reasons other than holidays. Caring for old or infirm family members was a significant
reason for emigrant women returning home, and they sometimes
stayed for lengthy periods. Eileen left her husband working in
Morecambe and took her young daughter back to Wexford in order
to nurse her sick mother:

> My mother became ill and I went home when Kathleen was a baby. Bill
> said: "Stay as long as you like." And I did, I didn't come back until
> Kathleen was five! I used to come back and forth to visit him. (Eileen,
> b. 1927, Co. Wexford)

Childbirth was another reason for some women to return to their
family in Ireland. Patriotism and a desire to be with their family in
familiar surroundings at an apprehensive time were the reasons
given for Irish women returning to Ireland to give birth:

> The eldest one was born in Ireland 'cause I went back to have him. I
> was afraid, you know, so I went back to have him amongst me own.
> I was more familiar with Ireland, ye know what I mean? And I thought
> I'd be safer over there, which was all nonsense. (Barbara, b. 1935,
> Co. Donegal)

> My daughters were both born in Ireland and I think it was really
> important for me that they were born there. They were Irish you see.
> (Eileen, b. 1927, Co. Wexford)

The death of parents was another life-cycle stage which affected women's pattern of visiting Ireland. Some women continued to visit but expressed regret that things had changed whilst for others, especially if all their brothers and sisters had emigrated, it marked the end of 'going home':

> There's nothing there, you know, after my father and mother died, the nostalgia, it was terrible. They were such happy days that we had there and it's all gone; finished! No, I never wanted to go back. (Mary, b. 1917, Co. Mayo)

Most women in the sample have kept in regular contact with their families, in Ireland and throughout the world, since emigration. The following recollection shows the typical means by which Irish emigrants and their families have kept in touch, and how they continue to do so:

> Me mother only stopped writing about two years before she died. She used to write about everything, you know. Me sister in Australia referred to mum's letters as 'the usual list of obituaries' because she always put in the people who'd died. I missed her letters a lot, oh yeah ... Me brother in London, he buys the local [Irish] paper and he'll ring me telling me about such a house up for sale, or land and everything. He knows everything that's going on locally. He keeps in touch that way, with the local paper. It's something I don't get but I don't need it because we go over so often and I'm in communication on the phone. Me brother is on the phone now in the homeplace. (Annie, b. 1929, Co. Cavan)

The experiences of Irish women in Lancashire between 1922 and 1960 again contradict the conclusions of Ide O'Carroll's research in America in which she stated: 'Irish women turned their backs on Ireland' and 'the rejection of family life was a major theme in the story of Irish emigrants to the U.S.A.'.[3] Conversely, the main conclusion of this chapter is that regular and frequent contact was usually maintained between Irish emigrant women in Lancashire and their families in Ireland. Furthermore, emigrant women generally welcomed this contact and often made sacrifices in order to sustain it.

Notes

1. Ide O'Carroll, *Models for Movers*, 1990, p. 145.
2. *Reports of the Commission on Emigration and other Population Problems 1948–1954*, [Pr. 2541], 1956, para. 313.
3. Ide O'Carroll, *Models for Movers*, p. 145.

CHAPTER FOUR

Religion

Religion and the family have already been identified as the two major recurring themes in every respondent's life history. The last two chapters have begun to show the continuing significance of the family on Irish women's lives after emigration and here the influence of religion on emigrant women's lives is investigated. The depth of information contained in oral life histories provides an ideal source for discovering the nature and extent of women's religious practices before and after they left Ireland and discerning whether or not any general changes or continuities in practice were apparent after emigration. Oral testimony is particularly useful because it gives an insight into women's motivation to practice religion and so the reasons for any identified patterns of religious practice are also provided.

The sample of respondents comprised of 39 Catholics and 1 Baptist. The predominance of Catholics within the sample was unintentional but largely inevitable. The religion of the respondents was not a criteria of the recruitment process and the religious composition of the sample was accidental. Steps were taken, however, to ensure that the sample was not biased towards women who were still practising any religion.[1] A majority of Catholic respondents was to be expected since most of Southern Ireland's population were (and still are) Catholic. In 1961, almost 95% of people in the Republic of Ireland were Catholics.[2]

Robert Kennedy has suggested that Irish Catholic emigrants were less likely to conform to the rules of their Church than were Irish Catholics who stayed at home:

> The most disaffected Irish Catholics were most likely to be found among the Irish abroad than at home. Those who were most willing to go along with the conventional expectations of their church were also the ones more likely to remain in Ireland, to accept the large family ideal of Catholic teaching and to marry early enough in life to turn the ideal into actuality.[3]

Kennedy's general claim can only be supported or questioned, not verified or refuted, by any evidence raised in this small sample. Nevertheless, the investigation of emigrant women's religious practices in this chapter, along with their personal lives and relationships in the next, can find out how far the claim is true of the emigrant Catholic women in this study.

Religion in the women's homes in Ireland
prior to emigration

Most of the respondents grew up in an environment where religious rituals and imagery were commonplace. Irish Catholic homes were decorated with pictures and statues of saints and, in pride of place over the mantlepiece, the obligatory Sacred Heart of Jesus:

> We had big statues of Our Lady, and the Child of Prague, and a big picture wi' all our names on it of the Sacred Heart; and the Sacred Heart lamp burning in front of the picture, you know. We had a huge big one o' St Patrick killing the snakes. The place was full o' them. (Barbara, b. 1935, Co. Donegal)

The practice of dedicating the Irish Catholic family to the Sacred Heart was widespread by the middle of the twentieth century. It involved a ceremony where the priest blessed the house and family in the presence of all family members and everyone present signed a document containing the consecration prayer. This was placed on the wall with a large picture of the Sacred Heart under which a lamp was permanently lit.

16. The Sacred Heart of Jesus, a familiar image in Irish Catholic Homes.

The Family Rosary was another well-established ritual in most Catholic homes in Ireland. It was recited every evening and all the family had to be in attendance. The oral evidence indicates that Irish mothers could use the timing of the Family Rosary to ensure that their husbands and older offspring returned home from the pub or the dance at a specified time which suggests that there could also have been a degree of family control behind this religious tradition. A favourite phrase of Fr Peyton, the priest whose crusade to popularise the family Rosary was phenomenally successful in Ireland, was: 'The family that prays together stays together' and many Irish mothers used the Rosary as a means of ensuring that they did:

> There used to be a little hut called the Penny Hop and that was all that we went to. If my sister and I went out to it we had tae be in the house again at ten o'clock to say the Rosary. Oh aye, and if ye didn't it was bedlam. (Noreen, b. 1913, Co. Donegal)

It is also evident that some people found this lengthy round of prayers tedious and sought humorous distractions:

> In our house my father said the Rosary and everybody had their own place to kneel ... The Rosary had funny sides to it as well. We'd lift the cat and put it on me mother's back and me mother'd giggle and my father'd give out, and then she'd say he should have been a monk. (Eileen, b. 1927, Co. Wexford)

17. Our Lady was a popular image on the mass-produced cards and medals which most Catholics carried on their person.

The accepted traditional view is that 'it is the mother who traditionally brings the family together to say the rosary and night prayers'[4] but the last testimony is only one of several examples in the oral history of Irish fathers leading the family prayers. It also shows that this woman's father was generally more religious than her mother and suggests that further research on the religiosity of Irish men might challenge the stereotype of Irish mothers being more devoted to religion than Irish fathers.[5]

OH MARY, give to all HOPE and PEACE!

Forget not the sorrows of Earth; cast a kind regard on those who suffer.

C. BULL   M.232   DUBLIN.

For some Irish children in the first half of this century home was literally a religious institution since it was the nuns, and to a lesser extent religious brothers, who managed and ran most of the country's welfare services including the children's homes. Not all children in the homes were orphans; a strict moral climate prevailed where illegitimate children were more likely to be hidden away in institutions than to be raised by their mothers in the community. Caroline's mother placed her in a Nazareth House Convent at the age of two, for reasons which were never disclosed to her, and she remained there until she was sixteen. Her memories depict an Irish institutionalised childhood which was marked by a regime of religious practices:

> As soon as you got outta bed in the morning you was on yer knees saying a prayer. This was about six

o'clock in the morning. Then you got dressed, you went downstairs and you went straight to Mass. And when that was over you went in and you had yer breakfast; another prayer before yer meal and a prayer after the meal. And then you went to school; we didn't go out to school, the nuns taught us ... One thing we all knew, and we all knew well, was our Catechism; I was good at that. I felt then it was prayer, prayer, prayer all the time; morning noon and night. Then at the school you had to go to church again for the Rosary, you know. Back again and have yer tea, and prayers again. Before ye went to bed we all had to kneel in this big hall and say another load o'prayers, go back up to bed and kneel at yer bedside. To me it was, you know, religion was drummed into ye then, it definitely was. But I mean, maybe that was the way it was, being brought up in a home, because nuns prayed all the time in them days. (Caroline, b. 1944, Co. Cavan)

Religion also influenced the diet of most Irish families. Prior to the changes which came about after the Second Vatican Council of 1962–65, Catholics were obliged to abstain from eating meat on Ash Wednesday and Good Friday (this still applies), and also every Friday. The oral testimonies indicate that priests in Ireland were particularly zealous in ensuring that their parishioners kept to this rule. Several women identified Friday to be a favourite day for the priest to visit their homes, and they commented that he would always examine their mother's cooking on this day. None of the Catholic respondents reported that they would have knowingly eaten meat on a Friday when they lived in Ireland and several of them reported feeling guilty and frightened if they had done so accidentally, no matter how small the morsel of meat had been:

Me grandmother used to make gorgeous soda bread, and if the crust was hard on the top, she'd put a little end of bacon on it ... She'd get a bit o' this fat and she'd rub it round the top of it. And I used to love to eat that little bit o' fat that had been rubbed around the cake. I swallowed it once, and then I remembered it was a Friday. And I can remember being so frightened! I thought something'd happen to me 'cause I ate that meat. (Maura, b. 1927, Co. Roscommon)

The one Protestant respondent recalled a much more secular home life in Ireland. Her memories of growing up in Athlone were of religion being confined to Sundays, a day which was taken up with services at the Baptist chapel and Sunday school attendance. She recalled that her father was an avid reader and there were many books in her house, particularly English classics such as Dickens and Jane Austen, but the mainstay of Protestant worship, the Bible, was absent. Significantly, she blamed the Catholic state for this:

> You see it was a very sad situation; you know you couldn't buy a Bible, we couldn't buy a Bible at all. At church if they were giving prizes it would be a Bible but they'd have to go over to England, or they'd go to the North, or they'd write away for them. There was no shops where you could go and buy a Bible. They [*Catholics*] had their own but they wouldn't provide a Protestant Bible. (Lily, b. 1929, Athlone)

Lily's Protestant home was the exception; all the other respondents (who were all Catholics), reported growing up in homes where they were surrounded by religious imagery, where the family regularly recited prayers, and where they did not eat meat on Fridays.

Religion in Irish emigrant women's homes in Lancashire

Only two Catholic women in this study discontinued the practice of decorating their homes with religious imagery once they left Ireland. One was Caroline, who had bitter memories of her institutionalised childhood and understandably did not want to be constantly reminded of the convent. The other was Barbara, who saw no necessity for pictures and statues in her marital homes in Glasgow and Lancaster because she did not attribute them with any religious significance. The more usual practice was of Irish women continuing to display Catholic imagery in their homes in Lancashire. Maureen grew up in an Irish home in Wigan and her recollections show that she and her Irish Catholic neighbours were surrounded by the same Catholic images as were their contemporaries in Ireland:

> Everybody had holy pictures. I can remember, in our big kitchen we had two big pictures. Did ye ever see that one: it was two little children playing near a river and the Guardian Angel? And then the other one was something the same. Then in the front room we always had one of Our Lady and one of Our Lord. And every so often, men used to come round selling them, and I can remember them showing them on the front room table and me mother buying two new ones. It was all holy pictures then. And upstairs we had [*St Theresa of*] the Little Flower. (Maureen, b. 1923, Wigan)

The Family Rosary appears to have endured less well outside Ireland. The practice was most likely to have been continued amongst families where the husband was an Irish Catholic and the wife did not work outside the home. For the majority of Irish emigrant women, the struggle of combining motherhood with employment outside the home (often working hours when their husband was at home to provide child-care) together with outside social distractions, left little time for the family to be together every evening. The memories of Noreen and Barbara are typical of the difficulties which faced many women who attempted to continue the tradition in England. Noreen's husband's income as a labourer on the railways was insufficient to keep them and their seven children and she worked evenings in old peoples homes for many years. This left herself and her husband with little time or energy with which to say the Rosary at night. Barbara recalled fighting a losing battle with the pub to attract her husband's attention in the evenings:

> It dropped away for years when we were bringing up the children for we never seemed tae have time to do much in that line. We never missed going to church and that but the Rosary seemed to drop away. (Noreen, b. 1913, Co. Donegal)

> We said the Rosary maybe for a year or so, but he was always in the pub anyway so ... you know, he was never at home. I was left there and that was it, you know. Well that's what breaks up families isn't it? You know, in Ireland in them days they all prayed together; it was just family life wasn't it? Once you come away from that there's too many distractions isn't there? Pubs and things like that. (Barbara, b. 1935, Co. Donegal)

The decline of the Family Rosary could possibly be due to migration from rural areas to towns more than emigration as such, but this explanation seems unlikely because the Dublin born women also remembered that the Family Rosary was regularly recited in their childhood homes. It was shown earlier in this chapter that the Family Rosary in Ireland was often remembered for its humorous distractions and it was regarded more as a necessary family duty than something of spiritual significance. This appears to be the most plausible explanation for its decline soon after emigration. The practice has been shown to have had a controlling element within families in Ireland and emigration to an environment where it was neither demanded nor expected, coupled with little belief in its spiritual merits, was the main reason why the ritual of the Family Rosary was largely discontinued after emigration.

Although there was a decline in the practice of the Family Rosary, the importance of prayer was still evident in many of the emigrant's lives at the time of their interviews. This quote was typical of many of the women's views:

> I think you just grew up and there was something in your mind was just driving you to say your prayers. I never now went on me knees in the morning, it was nearly always at night. Not just as I'd go into bed but sometime in the evening, when I'd be upstairs, I'd just kneel down and say a few prayers. It just comes more-or-less automatic now, and if

I didn't do it I'd think there was something missing. (Patricia, b. 1925, Co. Donegal)

On the whole, apart from the Family Rosary, religious images and prayer appeared to be as evident in Irish women's homes after emigration as they had been before.

The Church's influence on the diet of Irish families also appears to have survived emigration. This quote is typical of most of the Catholic women in this study in that it shows that most women continued to abstain from eating meat on Fridays after emigration and for as long as the Church laws existed; some women still feel uncomfortable with eating meat on Fridays now:

> Even when I was away from home I wouldn't eat meat on a Friday. I do eat it now, not often, but you're allowed to eat it now. (Oonagh, b. 1936, Co. Donegal)

The experiences of the women in this study suggest the continued influence of Irish Catholicism within their homes after emigration. Apart from the nightly saying of the Family Rosary, their homes in Lancashire were as identifiably Catholic as their parents' homes had been in Ireland. Symbols of their faith decorated the home, prayer was a daily practice, and the family diet was in accordance with the Church law.

Public religious practices before emigration

Attending Mass every Sunday and on the Church Holydays of Obligation was the practice of most Irish Catholics and of every Catholic respondent whilst they were living in Ireland. Children's behaviour in church was strictly controlled, not always by parents but by any adult within their vicinity. Young infants were rarely tolerated in the austere climate of Irish Masses in pre-Vatican II days and parents would often attend separate Masses whilst one of them minded the younger children at home, at least until they had an older daughter to leave in charge. In small parishes which only provided one Sunday Mass it was usually an older girl who had to miss Mass which, severe as it was, could be preferable to the drudgery of rural housework:

> When I was a child, when we were growing up and that, of course everybody couldn't go to Mass. If yer father and mother went, one of the girls would have to stay at home and get the dinner ready and that. There was no running water in the houses then and you had to go to the pump and get two buckets of water; you had to get that in and you had to wash the potatoes and put them on and have the dinner ready

when the rest all came in. And there were usually a baby in the house, so we used to take it in turns; one would stay at home on Sunday. (Siobhan, b. 1938, Co. Donegal)

None of the women in this study remembered any neighbours who completely rejected the Church's laws on Mass attendance but one woman noted the distinction which was made between the majority of the parish, who went to weekly Mass, and their neighbours who only went annually. The Church placed an emphasis on Catholics making their 'Easter Duties' and priests would ensure that even their most wayward parishioners conformed to this requirement. Rita's memory of her Wexford parish in the 1930s and 40s shows the self-righteous attitude that fellow parishioners displayed towards their less-regular Mass attenders:

They'd always come at the Easter Duty time, which was during Lent. Everyone had to go to Confession and Mass and make their Easter Duties. And the 'yearlings', as they called them, would show up that day. The yearlings would come, after they had been to Confession, and then you'd see them all shuffling up to Communion. And everybody would be sitting up there looking: "Oh, there's the yearlings going down." They went once a year. (Rita, b. 1930, Co. Wexford)

This quote also indicates that Mass attendance was clerically enforced and socially sanctioned in Ireland. The Catholic Church was very well organised in its control of Irish religious behaviour and employed missioners to reinforce the efforts of its regular clergy in maintaining the devotion of its members. Periodically, a Mission would visit every Irish parish with the intention of instilling fervour into the already practising Catholics and bringing back the lapsed ones. The specially trained missionary priests were noted for preaching ferocious sermons about the damnation which awaited sinners. The general impression gained from the Catholic respondents is that the Missions were associated with memories of fear; of the Missioners themselves and also of becoming eternally damned if they did not practise their religion fully. The Protestant respondent also recalled the terror which the Missions could bring to Protestant children in Athlone, where Catholic children zealously attempted to convert their Protestant contemporaries by using terror tactics:

The Catholics used to have what they called a Mission; every year there used to be a Mission for the men and there was a Mission for the women. But bedad when we'd be coming home from our Protestant school the Catholics would all meet us. They'd drag us into their church, and they'd kneel us down in front of these statues of Mary, and they'd kick the life out of you and say: "Say the Hail Mary! Say the Hail Mary!" It was shocking but that went on all the time; you just knew it happened. (Lily, b. 1929, Athlone)

The preceding quotes have indicated that, apart from religious devotion, coercion was also a possible explanation of the high levels of Mass attendance in Ireland. There is no doubt from the oral evidence that priests were generally feared in Ireland at this time and their authority was seldom questioned, no matter how severe or unjustified their actions were perceived to be:

> The priests were hard. If they didn't see you at Mass they'd come knocking on your door to see why you weren't at it. If you weren't there at Mass at 9 o'clock they'd come to your house and say: "Get yourself dressed for 11 o'clock Mass!" And they used to walk up with you up the lane. Oh aye yeah, they were very, very strict the priests in Ireland. (Sheila, b. 1923, Dublin)

Clerical influence extended beyond the directly religious sphere in Ireland and the undisputed control which priests exerted over their parishioners can only be appreciated when we see the unchallenged ways in which they infiltrated all areas of social and personal life. The next examples are typical of many similar instances which were recounted in the oral history:

> There was a dance hall right on the beach where we used to go on a Sunday night. And this big priest he waited till the dance was over, 'cause the couples used to all go along the shore for a walk after the dance; and I was among them as well. And many, many a time he used to go over and he used to drive us all over with a big blackthorn stick. And all you did was go for a walk! You just went for a walk but that wasn't allowed either. Ye'd see all the couples coming and him walking behind with this great big blackthorn stick. (Barbara, b. 1935, Co. Donegal)

> And of course the priest was the law. Same as if there was any violence like, between a married couple in Ireland, they would send for the priest. They wouldn't send for the police; the priest was the law. Everybody, you know Catholic families anyway, they sent for the priest. And everybody was frightened of him. Whatever it was; his word went! (Marion, b. 1932, Co. Mayo)

Most anti-clerical sentiments were expressed by the women from poorer Catholic families, who especially resented the practice of reading out from the pulpit the amount of donations which each family had contributed to the church:

> When you gave money to the church in Ireland all your names were

called out off the altar. That was wrong, because everybody knew how much you gave; that was awful. (Molly, b. 1931, Co. Longford)

Another reason why people might choose to attend Mass regularly was that it had a social as well as a religious function, especially in isolated rural areas where it provided a weekly time and place for all the neighbours to meet. A degree of both social class and gender segregation was evident in some churches:

In our church they had these seats where one aisle was women, the other aisle was men; women and men didn't mix then ... There was an area in the church where if ye paid for yer seat, if ye bought a seat in the church, ye sat in it and nobody else was allowed to sit in it. So all these wi' loads o' money would sit on that side o' the church. It was all wrong. When ye look back on it now it was very bad. (Breda, b. 1928, Co. Roscommon)

Respondents to the study also reported widespread gender segregation amongst parishioners after Mass had ended. It was customary after Mass for neighbours to greet each other and exchange news and gossip and this usually took place in single sex groups. Men, because they did not have the responsibility of caring for the children or preparing the dinner, could chat for a longer time at the chapel gates than women and then continue their socializing in the pub.

The oral evidence provided several reasons, other than the spiritual, for such strong adherence to regular attendance at Mass in Ireland. Fear of priests and of being snubbed by neighbours were major reasons why people conformed to the accepted behaviour of their largely homogeneous Catholic communities. Going to Mass also provided a regular opportunity for meeting and socialising with neighbours, especially in isolated rural communities.

Irish Catholic public religious practice was not confined to Mass attendance in church. Stations, Patterns and pilgrimages also figured prominently in many people's lives. Stations were particularly popular in the rural west of Ireland. They were a revival of the practice of saying Masses in private houses during Penal times, when Catholic churches were banned in Ireland and Britain. Parishioners took turns to host the Stations and they were obliged to feed and entertain the priest and all the neighbours after Confessions and Mass in the house were over. The priest would usually eat separately in the best room in the house and his departure signalled drinking and revelry by the rest of the gathering. It was customary to clean and decorate the house for the occasion and this involved a lot of work for the women of the house:

When I were growing up everybody had the Stations. He'd come round and say Mass. That was when ye got the house cleaned out. Ye had to

have it whitewashed an' all for the Stations. And then the priest's breakfast! It was the open fires then and you were trying to fry, and ye were
trying to do this and all the people were in, it was awful really! Oh it
was hard work. (Barbara, b. 1935, Co. Donegal)

The holding of the Stations was an obligatory requirement within
many rural Irish parishes and they appear to have been more important for women than men. The sacraments of Mass and
Confession, which most people already received regularly in church,
were not the most important aspects of the Stations for most women.
They put great effort into making their homes as clean and attractive
as possible and cooking meals for the occasion. So although they
were cloaked in religious ceremony, the Stations were more a display
of women's housekeeping skills, by which their respectability in the
community was measured. For both sexes the Stations were also a
symbol of Irish Catholic national identity because the tradition was
associated in popular memory with keeping the faith alive in Ireland
during the Penal times. Mass rocks[6] were commemorated with
annual Masses for the same reasons.

The land of Ireland is covered with sacred places which have often
been colonized by Christianity from ancient Pagan sites. By the
twentieth century the tradition of pilgrimages to Lough Derg in
Donegal, Croagh Patrick and the Marian Shrine at Knock in County
Mayo, and to numerous local holy wells was well established and
showed no signs of abating. Patterns, feast days of local saints, were
also an annual feature of most Irish parishes. The Church encouraged Catholics to make pilgrimages and granted indulgences to the
annual thousands who suffered the harsh endurances of climbing
Croagh Patrick or walking barefoot across the stones of 'St Patrick's
Purgatory' at Lough Derg. Some people, however, saw visits to holy
places as mainly social occasions and others did not go at all:

> I remember walking to Knock when I was eight. A crowd of us went at
> night, and it was about fifteen miles. We used to bring bread and tea
> and sugar ... Arragh sure it wasn't for the goodness of our soul we went,
> it was just an adventure to go. We used to go every year; we sort o'
> looked forward to it. (Maura, b. 1927, Co. Roscommon)

Religion permeated the daily lives of Catholics in Ireland but the
memories of Lily, the sole Protestant woman in this oral history,
demonstrate many differences between Catholic and Protestant lives
in Ireland. Her home was devoid of religious imagery and she was
brought up to regard religious statues and icons as evidence of
Catholic idolatry. Religious observances in her home were confined
to Sundays but they took up the whole of that day. Throughout

18. Pilgrims at Croagh Patrick, Co. Mayo, c. late 1940s. Reproduced courtesy of the National Library of Ireland.

Lily's testimony there is a poignant sense of the isolation which many Protestants in Southern Ireland must have felt at this time. Athlone had been a garrison town in her father's time but, after independence, the departure of the British soldiers depleted its Protestant community and the congregations of minority faiths such as hers had to combine in order to make even Sunday services viable:

> There was a small Baptist chapel near us and we attended there. Mind you we were the only family in the town who were Baptists. There was Methodists and Church of Ireland ... Oh yes, and one other man who had one son, they were Baptists; but that was all. We used to depend on other people coming along, you know, from the Methodists. And we'd go to the Methodists for special meetings. We always went to the chapel on a Sunday. In the summertime it would be in the morning and evening, and we used to have to go to Sunday School as well. The pastor and his wife had a family of three ... they all used to come to our house for dinner on a Sunday after church ... They'd all come and spend the day with us because it was too far to go home. The pastor travelled round different churches. (Lily, b. 1929, Athlone)

The recollections of religious practices in Ireland show how extensive Catholic practices were but there is less mention of a spiritual than a social dimension in them. The impression given by most of the Catholic respondents is that when they were practising their religion in Ireland, they were doing so mainly to conform to social norms. Lily's memories also provide no evidence that she gained any spiritual value from chapel and Sunday school attendance, rather that Sundays provided an opportunity for a declining, far-flung minority community to show solidarity.

Religious practices of emigrants in Lancashire

Lily attended chapel less frequently in Lancashire than she had done in Ireland although it was important to her that she married in, and her children were instructed in, the Baptist tradition. Her experience suggests that Protestant religious behaviour in Southern Ireland was influenced by Catholics. An antipathy towards Catholicism is a prevalent feature of her life-history narrative and once she no longer had to prove the validity of her minority faith in a Catholic society she relaxed her observances:

> There was a Zion Baptist church in Morecambe. We attended it. We were married there and the kids went to Sunday school there. I went a few times before I was married. We got married there and I didn't go anymore for a while. Then when the kids came along I just sent them up there to Sunday school. You'd think, well that was your church and that was it. (Lily, b. 1929, Athlone)

All of the thirty nine Catholic women had attended weekly Mass in Ireland and only four of them no longer went to weekly Mass at the time of their interview. It is worthwhile investigating Caroline, Siobhan, Barbara and Bridget's reasons for lapsing from Catholic practices. Caroline, whose unhappy memories of childhood in a convent orphanage have already been noted, spent her adult years trying to rebel against a religion which she remembered being forced on her as a child. At the time of interview, she attended Mass occasionally and she ensured that her children were christened Catholics, although she did not send them to Catholic schools. Ironically, she spent her working life in convents and had still not shaken off Catholicism's hold on her:

> I swore when I was in the home that when I left nobody'll tell me to go to church again. Yes I did; I said that even when I was in the home: "When I leave here nobody will ever tell me to go to church again. I will go if I want to go, when I'm ready to go!" I didn't even bring my kids

up to be Catholics. I didn't because of all that's probably happened to me Sharon. And I didn't want them to go to a Catholic school because I didn't want religion thrown down their throats. I must admit, I have regretted it in later years; but then I thought I was doing the right thing. But they were christened Catholics and they did make their communion. But they don't go to church and sometimes I feel sad about that. I mean I don't go – I do go now and again, that never left me you know. There's Paddy [*her husband*] who goes all the time. (Caroline, b. 1944, Co. Cavan)

Siobhan attended weekly Mass in both Ireland and Lancashire throughout the years covered in this history. When she was interviewed she was caring for two disabled sons and her invalid husband and she did not go to Mass any more. Her history relates that she went to Mass in Ireland because everybody else went; as a single woman in Lancashire, she worked with another Irish Catholic woman in a public house and her paternalistic employer ensured that they both attended Sunday Mass; she married an Irish Catholic man and she was obliged to accompany him to Mass. So, even though she appeared to be a practising Catholic for most of her life, this was because of external pressures rather than personal conviction. Only in comparatively recent years did she have the freedom to choose not to be a practising Catholic:

Oh you went [*to Mass*] in Ireland; oh yeah, you definitely went! And I always went when I first come over here. I don't go now. I went with me husband till he was ill; he always went. But I don't go now. A priest comes to me lads here every first Friday. Oh they were all christened Catholics and brought up Catholics. Me husband was a Catholic and I was a Catholic. (Siobhan, b. 1938, Co. Donegal)

Barbara also continued to attend weekly Mass after emigration and stated that her divorce ten years ago was the cause of her lapsed attendance:

I used to never miss Mass when I came here first. I went to Mass up until I got divorced. And then I fell away. I thought, well I did wrong, you know. But the priest, he said that's all nonsense. He comes round and he says: "You should go back to Mass." It's just that I'm so long away from it now, it'd take me a long time getting back into it again. (Barbara, b. 1935, Co. Donegal)

If this quote is read in isolation, Barbara is seen as a once-devout Catholic who lapsed because she felt guilty after breaking one of the Church laws on marriage. However, since she had not remarried, she could still continue to be a full member of the Church, should she so wish. Elsewhere in her interview, Barbara questioned the spiritual validity of several Catholic traditions, such as pilgrimage and miraculous cures, and she chose not to display any religious imagery in her home in Lancashire. In the next chapter it will also be shown that she also defied the Church's rule on contraception. It is only by considering her whole life history that another explanation can be suggested: she was always a reluctant Catholic and divorce offered her an excuse to leave the Church. It is significant that her ex-husband was a practising Catholic throughout their marriage, and even more significant that she spoke of returning to the Church in the context of being urged by the priest to do so.

Bridget ceased to attend Mass after the death of her husband five years ago. She fell out with her parish priest after he did not mention her husband's name during a memorial Mass she had paid for. Prior to this, she presented as a devout Catholic woman in Ireland and England. Once again, however, her history records that her devotion was not always because of free choice. When Bridget first came to England in 1950 she was obliged to attend Mass in order to please her immediate employer, who was also an Irish woman. This quote shows that she was not so diligent when it was left to her own conscience. Dan, her Co. Roscommon husband, was a very devout churchgoing Catholic, which she attributed to his rural origins, and she contrasted his piety with her own attitude:

> Well where I worked, you see, there was a matron there, she was Irish; oh a bitch, a bitch! And she made us go to Mass. But I never bothered after; sometimes I'd go and sometimes I wouldn't. But Dan, God rest his soul, used to be very good-living. God Almighty! He used to say to me: "Oh why don't you get yourself down to Mass?" He never in his life missed Mass Sharon. I'm not boasting with lies, it's the Gospel truth; he never missed of a Sunday ... All country men are like that. In the city they're not bothered I don't think; they don't bother about it in the city in Ireland but the country people are dedicated to their religion ... He used to have a Rosary bead hanging on the bed, you know, and sometimes, when I'd hoover, it would drop and I wouldn't hear it like. Before he'd go into bed at night he'd be looking for that bead! He'd say: "Mam, why don't you kneel down and say a few prayers?" I used to say: "Cop yourself on dad and get into bed before you get pneumonia; are you crackers or what?" A very good-living man he was. He never, never missed in his life." (Bridget, b. 1930, Cork City)

Bridget did not reject the Catholic Church completely. She still attended Mass, periodically rather than regularly, and she sent money to her late husband's parish in Ireland in order for Masses to be said for him.

The remaining Catholic women in the sample were attending

weekly Mass at the time of their interviews and all but one of them had an unbroken pattern of regular attendance throughout their lives. The exception was Lena. She emigrated to England from Co. Galway in 1946. She recalled that she lapsed from being a regular churchgoer for a time when she lived in England as a young single woman but since returning to live in rural Ireland in 1982 she has conformed to her neighbours' behaviour and attended Mass every Sunday. Marriage to an Irish Catholic man was one reason why she started attending Mass again in Lancashire, and also the respectability which having churchgoing parents gave to her children whilst they attended Catholic schools:

> I went to church for a while after I went over to England, then I got outta church for a long time. And when I got married I remember Kevin doing a general Confession and he made me go and do the same ... You went to church quite often really, especially after you were married; 'cause your children went to a Catholic school and you'd be disgraced. Once, when my son was five, he came out with this very bad word at school; he told somebody to 'F' Off ... And the teacher wrote me this letter and she said she knew it didn't come from our house ... If you didn't go to church you'd be sort o' disgraced; they'd say: "Oh what can ye expect?" Ye know. So you wouldn't show your kids up by not going to church. (Lena, b. 1930, Co. Galway)

It is significant that all five of the women who admitted to lapses in their Catholic practices were married to churchgoing Irish Catholic men. They described their husbands as being more devout than them and at times only kept up Catholic observances because of their husband's wishes. These examples, along with those earlier recollections in this chapter, of devout fathers reciting the Family Rosary, certainly challenge the notion that 'Irish women would appear to be more religious than Irish men'.[7] More research into the religiosity of Irish men is clearly needed.

The majority of women in this sample, that is the thirty four remaining after taking into account the one Protestant woman and the five Catholic women who admitted to lapses in their religious practices, said that they had continued to practise their Catholic faith, including attending Confession and weekly Mass, uninterrupted throughout their lives:

> I've never missed Mass, only on the birth of my first child and through flu; about four times in my life. (Eileen, b. 1927, Co. Wexford)

Although a total of five respondents lapsed from Catholicism at some time in their lives, during the years studied here, only Caroline and Lena did not go to Mass every Sunday. Thirty seven out of the thirty nine Catholic respondents, therefore, were regularly practising Catholics during the years covered by this study.

Coercion from employers, marriage to churchgoing Irish Catholics, and promoting a respectable family image when their children were attending Catholic schools have already been cited as reasons for Irish women continuing to practise Catholicism in Lancashire but more explanations are also evident.

Lily, a Protestant, moved from a Catholic-dominated society to a Protestant one and for her, emigration signalled an end to the overwhelming influence of Catholicism on her life. The reverse situation existed for Irish Catholic women. They left a Catholic society for a Protestant one, but the Church took steps to ensure that they adhered to the faith after emigration. Annie, who left Co. Cavan to train as a nurse in Ashton-Under-Lyne in 1949, was one of several women who remembered her parish priest issuing her with a letter of introduction which was to be given to the local priest at her destination:

> I don't know when it started but by 1948 every Sunday, off the altar in Ireland, ye'd hear the priest saying: "And another crowd has gone off to England!" But they didn't say very nice things about it because they felt they were going off to dens of iniquity and selling their souls and all that: "And if any more of ye have any ideas about going, yous'll come and yous'll get a letter from us before you go!" I had to be doing the right thing; I couldn't cope with not doing the right thing and I had a letter of introduction. I suppose it was a good thing in a way ... We came with a letter from our priest in Ireland and you went and gave that letter to the priest here. (Annie, b. 1929, Co. Cavan)

Church organisation was also used to maintain the allegiance of Catholic nurses in Lancashire:

> The Catholic priest always used to come and see us. They notified them when there was Catholic nurses and he used to come down and visit us and everything. And he used to tell the matron that she had to let us go to Mass. Because you see, Mass was only on Sunday mornings then, there was no evening Mass and there was no late night Saturday Mass you could go to. So you had to go to either 9 o'clock or 11 o'clock, and if you hadn't the day off she would give you a split turn in the morning. They used to do that with us all. (Theresa, b. 1928, Co. Roscommon)

Catholic parishes in Lancashire could also provide social facilities which particularly lessened the isolation experienced by women who came to towns where they had no relatives:

> When I came here to Morecambe I didn't know nobody. I used to go

down to St Mary's church and there was a priest there, Fr Clayton, and I remember him taking me round to the church hall and there was girls playing table-tennis there. And he introduced me to them and I sort of got to know them and that was it. (Maura, b. 1927, Co. Roscommon)

Catholic parish halls and schools were also the venues where women reported taking their children for Irish dancing and music lessons. Bridget was a practising Catholic in Ireland and Lancashire throughout the years of this study but not at the time of interview. One reason why she kept in contact with her local Catholic parish in Lancaster was that it provided places where she could keep up her Irish step dancing:

When I first come to England I brought all me step dancing medals with me. Oh God, I was a great dancer Sharon. I got two lovely trophies. I danced in Dublin, Stephen's Green, all over, years ago. I used to be in concerts ... In Lancaster I used to do it down in the Catholic Club. And I was teaching 'em down there in St Peter's school years ago. (Bridget, b. 1930, Cork city)

The influence of a priest in Lancashire enabled one woman to gain entry to her chosen profession. Molly came from Co. Longford to live with her sister in Lancaster in 1951 with hopes of becoming a nurse:

I came over to my sister and I met Fr Kelly and I told him I'd like to be a nurse. And he said: "Well I'm going up and I'll see the matron tomorrow and ask if you can be on the next batch." ... So I went nursing to the infirmary. (Molly, b. 1931, Co. Longford)

The previous example could suggest that priests in Lancashire had as much authority beyond their spiritual role as they had in Ireland but it would appear that they exercised a more benign form of authority in Lancashire that they did in Ireland. The Catholic women in this study unanimously agreed that they found priests in Lancashire to be generally less authoritarian and more approachable than the ones they encountered in Ireland:

There was a difference between the priests over here and in Ireland. Oh yeah, I wasn't frightened of 'em anymore; they treated you like a human being. (Bridget, b. 1930, Cork city)

The marked difference in attitude between Catholic priests in Ireland and Lancashire can not be explained by a difference in their nationality since many of the priests whom Irish women encountered in Lancashire were Irish themselves. The Catholic Church in England did not hold the allegiance of the majority of the population as it did in Ireland and its priests had to earn the respect of parishioners. Clerical coercion was a factor in maintaining Catholic worship in Ireland but it was not usually a reason for Irish women remaining practising Catholics in Lancashire.

Just as it had in Ireland, Mass also served as a meeting place for the Irish in Lancashire and men in particular appear to have continued the tradition of gathering outside the church for a chat with their countrymen. Maureen remembered her coalminer father meeting up with men from his native county Mayo after Mass in Wigan in the 1930s and '40s:

> Me father, you see, he'd always go to 11 o. clock Mass and then they'd talk outside the chapel, and they'd have a pint then. That was the only day he used to have a pint because he'd be always working. And they were all from round his own place, you know; all from round Charlestown. (Maureen, b. 1923, Wigan)

Molly also remembered the custom of Irish men meeting outside church being carried on in Lancaster in the 1950s, but she attributed a more patriotic reason to the tradition

> When I first came over, the cathedral in Lancaster used to be packed, because there was a lot of Irish here. A lot o' them in the cathedral was Irish. I remember it used to be really good, because ye'd come out and all the Irishmen would be all standing across at the wall. That's the custom of Irishmen coming out o' church, d'ye know that? Have you ever heard the story of that? Years ago, you know, when they were killing the Catholics, going back hundreds of years ago. They were killing them here as well. In Ireland then you couldn't say Mass, you couldn't do anything. They used to watch. They used to come out o' Mass and stand at the door watching to see if anybody was coming; and they kept up that custom. And I read it in a book that this is why all Irishmen … even they do it at home now; you know at home they're all outside? And it was the same here in Lancaster. I remember coming out and all the Irishmen in long rows, all standing right along. Along that wall from the cathedral it was all Irishmen, all standing there talking. Oh they'd stand for an hour talking. (Molly, b. 1931, Co. Longford)

Molly's explanation illustrates her association of Catholicism with being Irish and maintenance of Irish national identity was also a contributory factor to the continuing practice of Catholicism amongst the Irish in Lancashire. The extensive contact which emigrant women maintained with their families in Ireland would also encourage continuity of traditional religious practices, since any lapses would not go undetected by the rest of the family.

Conclusions

Catholicism in Ireland was not only church based, it extended into every sphere of life and affected Protestants as well as Catholics. It appears that for some Protestants at least, the practice of their religion in post-independence Ireland was undertaken more for political than religious reasons; to uphold their minority identity in a state in which Catholicism was increasingly pervading all spheres of life. Protestants were probably less motivated to show their allegiance to their Church in England than they had been in Catholic Ireland.

There is evidence of a strong continuity of Irish Catholic practices amongst emigrant women in Lancashire. The reasons for religious conformity after emigration were often similar to those which accounted for such behaviour in Ireland but their emphasis changed. Whilst coercion can be seen to have been a major factor in Ireland, it was not so much in Lancashire, where priests were no longer feared and all the surrounding community were not practising Catholics. However, there is evidence that the Catholic Church did exert some measure of control over Irish women in Lancashire, as in the practice of Irish parish priests issuing emigrants with letters of introduction to be given to priests in Lancashire. Young Irish nurses were also targeted by priests and arrangements for their Mass attendance were ensured. Catholic employers and associates of single Irish women could also regulate their religious behaviour. Catholic parishes also offered social facilities which were an attraction for some emigrants. The influence of family was still a very important factor in the continuance of religious behaviour after emigration as many women kept in regular contact with relatives in Ireland. Having churchgoing parents also gave their children respectability in Catholic schools and this was a motive for some mothers to attend Mass. Some Irish Catholic husbands also ensured the religious fidelity of their wives in Lancashire. For the majority of the respondents, who have adhered to their religious practices not just in Ireland and Lancashire during the years studied here but throughout their lives since, the aforementioned secular reasons for conformity to religious practices have largely ceased to affect them. They no longer have parents, or in some cases husbands, to please; or children attending Catholic schools; or coercive employers; or need the facilities of the Catholic Church for introducing them to other people in a strange community. They have, however, demonstrated a belief that devotion to the Catholic Church will bring them salvation.

The findings of this research so far do not support Robert Kennedy's claim that 'the most disaffected Catholics were most likely to be found among the Irish abroad'.[8] They were not likely to be found in Lancashire at least. Religious practices are, however, not the only measures of Catholic belief. Catholic Church doctrine also influenced Irish women's personal relationships, as will be seen in the next chapter.

Notes

1. These steps are detailed in chapter one.
2. Tom Inglis, *Moral Monopoly*, 1987, p. 12.
3. Robert E. Kennedy, Jr., *The Irish*, 1973. p. 193.
4. Tom Inglis, *Moral Monopoly*, 1987, p. 68.
5. For a comprehensive description of the stereotypical Irish Catholic mother, see Tom Inglis, *Moral Monopoly*, 1987, pp. 187–214.
6. When Catholic worship was prohibited during penal times, Catholics often continued to gather for Mass in secret. Houses of Catholic gentry were sometimes used in England, particularly in Lancashire. In rural Ireland, parishioners often gathered in remote mountainous areas, where the priest would use a large rock as the altar and these rocks became known as Mass rocks.
7. Tom Inglis, Moral Monopoly, p. 68.
8. Robert Kennedy, *The Irish*, p. 193.

CHAPTER FIVE

Personal relationships

Documentary evidence of people's personal relationships in former times is scarce but the use of oral history is providing a growing literature on this topic.[1] This investigation of Irish emigrant women's personal and sexual relationships will compare their experiences in Ireland and Lancashire and determine how far this particular area of their lives was affected by emigration. The importance of the family and Catholicism on Irish women's lives have already been shown and the influence of these two factors on emigrant women's personal and sexual relationships will also be assessed.

Personal experiences before emigration

The country where most of the respondents grew up and left as young adults was a sexually repressive society. Throughout the first forty years of Irish independence, successive politicians and Church leaders demonstrated an obsessive preoccupation with protecting the Irish masses from sexual immorality, as defined by the Catholic state. The Censorship of Publications Act of 1929 and its amendment in 1946 were solely concerned with prohibiting material of a sexual nature including any literature promoting birth-control. Section 17 of the Criminal law Amendment Act of 1935 banned the advertizing, importation and sale of contraceptives in the state. In his minority report to the Commission on Emigration and other Population Problems, Dr Cornelius Lucey, who was the Bishop of Cork, summed up the Irish ideal of marriage:

> The primary purpose of marriage, in the natural order of things, is the birth of children. This is not to say that people do not, or may not, marry for other reasons; it is but to say that the most fundamental reason, the one to which all others must yield precedence is the raising of a family ... The ideal family is the large family ... The use-and so the manufacture and sale-of contraceptives must be regarded as in all circumstances against the Moral Law. It is as wrong for married persons as it is for those not married at all ...[2]

The majority report of the Commission was alarmed that there was a trend towards smaller families in Ireland, even though Irish family sizes were declining far less than in other countries in Western Europe. Furthermore, the Commission, which was made up of 22 men and just 2 women, could find no valid reasons why Irish women should consider that having large numbers of children might be detrimental to their well-being:

> ... we can find no support for the view that, apart from the increased risk associated with frequent child-bearing, large families have a deleterious effect on the general health of mothers ... it would be unreasonable to assume that our family pattern imposes an undue strain on mothers in general. [3]

The 'increased risk associated with frequent child-bearing' was of little consequence to the Commission but it was a harsh fact of life for many Irish women whose marital relationships were overshadowed by the ever-present possibility of yet another pregnancy.

The prevailing moral climate was one of rigid censorship which only accepted the Catholic teaching that sex was restricted to married couples for the sole purpose of producing children. Outside of marriage sex had no purpose, and consequently no legitimate place in Irish society. The taboo on sex outside of marriage would appear to have been very strong in Southern Ireland and even talk about sex was forbidden in most Irish families. Most women reported being ignorant of sexual matters during their youth. Siobhan's recollection is typical in that it illustrates a complete lack of sex education combined with being instilled with a fear that contact with the opposite sex was sinful:

> There was no such thing as teaching the facts o' life. Most parents wouldn't talk about it because they weren't told when they were young and it was an embarrassing situation. You probably got a clip round the ear if ye asked, ye weren't allowed to ask questions like that. So you weren't told but ye sorta got yer own instinct that it was wrong, you know, to have sex outside of marriage. But the priest used to preach about it, even though we didn't know what sex was, especially at the Mission. The Missioners used to come and a whole crowd of us went to the church and we'd probably meet someone to walk in with. I remember once we were at the Mission and they preached at the altar "When you boys and girls go outta here tonight walk straight home, otherwise ye'll burn wi' brimstone!" and all that. And I remember we were all so frightened that we all looked at the lads and they went one way and we went another way ... They sorta preached like that. They didn't say we were not to have sex or anything, just to walk home with a boy was out!
> (Siobhan, b. 1938, Co. Donegal)

Even when mothers gave birth at home, as most Irish women did, particularly in rural areas, the birth and even the pregnancy was generally kept well hidden from the other children in the family.

Boys were often no more aware of sexual matters than girls. Molly was born in Longford in 1931 and her Donegal born husband Eamonn was present during part of her interview. When Molly stated that before she was married: 'I was ignorant about the facts o' life', her husband added:

> Both of us were. I was married before I knew! ... You never even noticed your mother was expecting. No, that last brother of mine was born when I was fifteen and I never knew my mother was expecting! I wonder why that was? The children now know everything, they're far too bloody clever. (Eamonn, b. 1932, Co. Donegal)

Eamonn's incredulity at the extent of his youthful sexual ignorance was shared by most of the respondents, none of whom remembered being told how babies were conceived or born.

The strength of the family ideal in Irish society meant that the behaviour of individual members reflected upon the reputation of the whole family and upholding the good name of the family was an important motivation for conforming to socially acceptable behaviour. Despite being told little or nothing about sex, and even less about birth control, most respondents reported that the greatest shame they could have brought upon their families in Ireland was to have become pregnant outside of marriage. Eileen was one of several respondents who remembered pregnant brides not being allowed to marry in daylight with the usual Nuptial Mass, instead they were shamed by having to avail of a clandestine wedding at night time at the back of the church:

> I'm talking of the 1930's and '40s. If you were pregnant and you wanted to be married, you went at night time and got married in the back o' the church. That did happen and I thought it was strange. (Eileen, b. 1927, Co. Wexford)

The social stigma of being a pregnant bride was preferable to the harsh attitudes which were shown to illegitimate mothers. A minority of single mothers did continue to live at home with their children but they were an affront to the dominant values of Irish society who were, at best, barely tolerated and more usually reviled:

> I remember there was this girl and she had two children and she was an outcast. An outcast! She was a 'bad woman', oh yeah. (Molly, b. 1931, Co. Longford)

Emigration or incarceration in homes for unmarried mothers were more usual practices since they concealed illegitimacy in Ireland:

> The girls that had illegitimate babies, I think they had them out o'

ignorance because they weren't told anything ... If a girl had a child and she wasn't married they treated her worse than if she had took a gun and murdered half a dozen people. It was a thing that was never forgotten, and probably wouldn't be to this day ... Their mother and father usually threw them out. If they didn't come over here [England] there was a place called the County Home over there where young expectant mothers went. And I heard people talk that they were treated worse than criminals in it. And then, when the baby was born, the mother and child had to stay in that home until one of her parents and a priest signed her out. And some o' them people was never signed out; they had to stay there for years. (Siobhan, b. 1938, Co. Donegal)

Infanticide was the ultimate way of hiding illegitimate births and the oral evidence indicates that it was carried out not just by desperate women alone but with the assistance of their families. It is impossible to determine how many unfortunate women resorted to this practice but Irish society's harsh response to single mothers undoubtedly contributed to making infanticide more prevalent than it would have been in a more tolerant climate:

Some women had children and they got rid o' them, they buried them in different places. They were frightened to tell so they had to. And the families helped too, in case they brought a bad name on the family. (Molly, b. 1931, Co. Longford)

They buried them at night. Do you know where they buried them? Well they took them into the graveyard, but they didn't bury them in the graveyard, they buried them in a ditch by the side o' the graveyard. That's true. They buried them after it was dark at night. Say some lassie had a kid, it was taken away at night, it was taken away at night by two men and they dug a grave up at the edge o' the graveyard. That's true. 'Cause I know there's some buried where I came from. (Eamonn, b. 1932, Co. Donegal)

The traditional image of a desperate unmarried pregnant Irish woman resorting to emigration or infanticide is usually that of a woman alone, concealing her plight from her family. It would appear that this was not always the case. More research on this subject might reinforce what the oral evidence from this study suggests: that Irish families might have understood and accepted sexual indiscretions to a greater extent than was previously thought but that they colluded to hide them for fear of disapproval from the wider community.

Illegitimate children, as well as their mothers, were despised in Irish society. Caroline was raised in a Nazareth House convent where she was visited regularly by her mother but never told anything about her father. She recalled being made to feel ashamed about her illegitimacy in Ireland. She left the convent at the age of fifteen to work as a cleaner in a hospital but she was soon sacked from this job and incarcerated in yet another institution after an emotive reaction to being called a bastard by a staff nurse:

> I left there [*Nazareth House*] and I was one of the bad temperedest people that ye'd ever met! I think I was a very bitter person ... Anyway, I worked in the Mater Hospital and I remember I told one o' the nurses to eff off. One o' the nurses called me a bastard right? She was a staff nurse. And in them days to be called that! You knew what you were. Because I was one, wasn't I? For anybody to turn round and call you that in them days was a terrible thing. So I gotta hold o' this staff nurse by the head o' the hair and I swung her round the ward, you know, in front of all the patients. I said "Nobody calls me that and gets away with it!" Because it was something that you were sort o' brought up to be ashamed of, you know. And I was put in the Good Shepherd for that ... It was a big place, the Good Shepherd Convent. Part of it was girls that were sent in from outside, that got in trouble with the police; not serious crimes, probably just lost their way, you know. And there was a part for the poor girls that got themselves into bother [*pregnant*], you know. (Caroline, b. 1944, Co. Cavan)

While single mothers and their illegitimate children were shunned by Irish society, men were often given the benefit of the doubt if they chose not to admit that they had fathered illegitimate children:

> There might have been rumours going about but ye didn't know if it was the truth or not. There was no such thing as taking them for maintenance, or no such thing as them paying some money towards them or anything like that. They just never bothered. (Oonagh, b. 1936, Co. Donegal)

A sexual double standard can also be seen in the attitudes towards alcohol consumption amongst young people in Ireland. It was usual for both boys and girls to make a promise to abstain from alcohol at their Confirmation and 'the pledge', as it was known, lasted until they were twenty one. Although boys were seen as heroic if they kept the pledge, they were often excused for breaking it. It was, however, considered shameful for a girl to break the pledge:

> When you went for your Confirmation you took the pledge until you were twenty one. And if you broke the pledge you were treated as some sort of wicked criminal, you know. Most o' the boys did break it, but not women. That was something that ye kept till ye were twenty one. (Siobhan, b. 1938, Co. Donegal)

The inconsistent attitude to girls and boys drinking can be seen as an early introduction of girls into the sexual inequalities of Irish society. Whilst drunken lapses of morality were excuseable amongst males, women were charged with the full responsibility of, and subsequent blame for, sexual indiscretions.

Despite being warned in the home, church and classroom against 'company keeping' young Irish men and women did manage to meet socially and, ironically, Catholic Church activities often provided opportunity for courtship. Whilst young people's organisations and sodalities such as the Legion of Mary were segregated and designed to keep the sexes apart, weekly Mass and nightly prayers during the Rosary month of October provided a respectable excuse for meeting the opposite sex before young people were old enough to be allowed to go to dances:

> In them days your courting was more-or-less done going to church, you seen them on the way back from church. Because the parents were so strict then, you know. October was a good month because you used to say the Rosary and it was a good excuse to get out! And when we were older we started going to dances, you see, and we met them at dances. (Siobhan, b. 1938, Co. Donegal)

Parental approval appears to have been more important than personal attraction in determining whether or not a relationship progressed. No respondents reported continuing to meet a young man whom their parents disapproved of but several women ended relationships at their parents' insistence. Significantly, none of these women questioned their parents' judgement in the matter. Patricia stopped seeing her boyfriend in Donegal in the early 1940s after her postman father observed not her boyfriend's, but his family's drinking habits:

> I was going out with a chap from home for three years. At that time you'd just go out with them and you'd see them once a week or once a fortnight and that would be it. But I finished with him then 'cause there was a lot of drinking in his family and I was advised not to carry it on. Me father was delivering letters and he knew that his parents and grand-parents were, you know, very fond of beer drinking. At that time you seemed to take notice of your parents. (Patricia, b. 1925, Co. Donegal)

This last example reinforces the point made earlier, that the family ideal was so strong in Irish society that the reputation of individuals was never regarded in isolation but was reflected on the whole family; and vice-versa in Patricia's unfortunate boyfriend's case.

Irish girls grew into womanhood largely lacking any knowledge in sexual matters but very aware of the shame and stigma which was associated with pregnancy outside of marriage. They knew that pregnancy occurred through some sort of association with males but confusion and ignorance generally clouded their awareness of the sexual act until they had actually experienced it. Sheila had an illegitimate child in Dublin in 1947. She became pregnant at the age of twenty four after her first and only sexual encounter. She recalled that the birth of her son was a traumatic time when she had to endure cruelty from nurses in the maternity hospital and stave off attempts to force her to have the child adopted or hand him over to a married sister and her husband:

> It was terrible, absolutely! And the nurses would absolutely smack your face. Yes, they even threw the child at me in the hospital. And I cried. I cried and cried. They even sent the Social to the hospital for me to adopt him but I said "No, I'm keeping him." They wanted to know how I would keep him and I said I'd work ... Then me sister came to see me one day in the hospital. She was saying "Don't get it adopted, don't get it adopted. I'll take it." So I said "Nobody's getting him." I said I would work for him and I did. I worked for a Jew and I was allowed to bring the child. It was in a fish and chip shop and the child was allowed to be in the corridor in the pram where I could see him. (Sheila, b. 1923, Dublin)

Sheila's defiant determination to raise her son alone in Ireland survived the wrath of her family but not that of a priest. She was blissfully ignorant of the fact that she had transgressed the Catholic Church's rules but was rudely enlightened of them after her sister made her go to Confession. Soon after this incident she emigrated from Ireland:

> He threw me out of Confession 'cause I'd committed a mortal sin ... I was going to church all the time, even when the child was born. As a matter of fact I didn't understand the Church at first like, you know, because I went to Mass every Sunday and I received the Sacraments every Sunday. And then me sister said to me: "You shouldn't be going to Communion." I asked why, and she said: "You want to go to Confession and talk to the priest." I'm sorry I ever did! ... He just said to me: "Get out of this church! Get out of this church!" And he was really shouting. Do you know, my face was red when I came out of that Confession box; I thought everybody heard him outside ... He was an old priest; I'll never forget that priest as long as I live, I'll never forget him! I thought it was my fault, I shouldn't have had a baby ... Do you know? When that happened to me I thought I was going to get burned in Hell. I did, I always thought that. For nights and nights and nights I used to think about it and cry about it, you know ... I feel guilty all the time. When

I go into church I do talk to God and ask him why he's got me thinking like this all the time? (Sheila, b. 1923, Dublin)

Women like Sheila were stigmatised and, worse still, they internalised the shame which Irish society heaped upon them and yet, fifty years after she conceived her child, she revealed in her life history that she was still unaware of how she became pregnant and had never touched a man since. Her experience reinforces the earlier quote from Siobhan which suggested that it was often the most sexually naive Irish women who had illegitimate babies.

The two married women who had children before they emigrated both reported that even after marriage they did not know how babies were conceived or born. A few months after her marriage in Donegal in 1932, Noreen's married sister-in-law had to explain her condition:

When I was caught wi' me first child I didn't know what was wrong wi' me. I used to be sick every morning and I couldn't understand why. And it was me husband's sister told me. She says: "Ye silly sod, ye are pregnant?" (Noreen, b. 1913, Co. Donegal)

Ignorance and taboos clouded sexual knowledge generally in Ireland but homosexuality was particularly hidden. The overwhelming impression gained from the life histories is of extensive ignorance about homosexuality amongst young adults in Ireland. Maeve was in her early twenties and well advanced in her medical studies in Dublin when she first heard the word lesbians during a discussion with friends and she could not comprehend that such women existed:

I suppose I was about a fourth year medical student when, I remember, we were crossing the top of Grafton Street and somebody started talking about lesbians and I said "What's lesbians?" I'd never heard of a lesbian. They said "A love affair between two girls." I said "How the hell can you have a love affair between two girls?" I thought it was utter, complete rubbish. I didn't have a clue! (Maeve, b. 1917, Co. Tipperary)

Sean O'Ciarain's autobiography suggests that men in Ireland were often as unaware of the existence of homosexuals as women. He left Co. Mayo in 1947 to work as a potato picker in Scotland and it was here that he and several other young Irish labourers observed a gay man for the first time. Like Maeve, they were also puzzled by the concept of homosexuality:

A youngish red-haired man worked on a nearby farm and took to hanging around the bothies most evenings. The strange thing about this bloke was that he seemed to be far more interested sexually in the young lads than he was in the girls. This was something new to me, I had never come across a man like that before. I just did not know what to make of him, or how it was that he had his sexual priorities all wrong. I had never heard of the likes, neither had some of the others. [4]

The reaction of Sean and his colleagues was to chase the unfortunate youth and pelt him with stones and it is little wonder that homosexuality remained hidden in Irish society for many years.

Post-independence Ireland was a society where sexual knowledge was limited and relationships were strictly controlled. Sex was not promoted as a pleasurable experience. It was associated with sin and shame outside of marriage but after marriage it was to be endured for the procreation of children. Homosexuals and single mothers threatened the ideal family-centred Irish society and the comparatively few who were visible were despised; most were hidden. Most emigrant women were young, sexually naive adults when they left this sexually repressive society and their subsequent experiences after emigration will now be discussed.

Personal experiences after emigration

Several respondents recalled that they had found women in Lancashire to be more sexually aware than women in Ireland. Maura emigrated from Co. Roscommon in 1945 when she was eighteen. In 1946, whilst working as a chambermaid in Morecambe, she was shocked by the discussions of her workmates:

I did see a big difference between the way boys and girls were in England and Ireland. Because it was sorta drilled into you so much [in Ireland], to respect your body, in case you got pregnant, you know. But when I came here and I was listening to these two girls that came to work from Liverpool. When I used to hear them talking and things it was alien to me, you know, about what they got up to when they went out. (Maura, b. 1927, Co. Roscommon)

Maura's reaction was to distance herself from the Liverpool women and although she went to dances in Morecambe, she socialised with other young Irish women who conformed to her view of respectability. She subsequently met and married a Catholic from Co. Kerry.

Only one respondent recalled having sex outside marriage after she emigrated, and she was also unfortunate enough to become pregnant. She was more fortunate than Sheila from Dublin in that her pregnancy resulted from an affectionate relationship, but her story illustrates how similar her feelings were to those of Sheila. She also internalised the shame and she sacrificed her own happiness because of her Catholic belief. Bernadette was in love with the father of her child when she became pregnant in Blackpool in 1945, but he was a divorced English Protestant and they could not have a Catholic wedding. He wanted them to be married in a registry office but in order to remain true to her faith she chose instead to have her son in a Catholic convent for unmarried mothers and raised him alone in Lancaster:

> I went through an awful lot, a terrible lot, not of anxiety but … Why didn't I marry him? and all this kinda thing. It was shocking. Terrible! … We were going to get married but he was divorced. Well I was walking along Blackpool prom one day, thinking of all this, you know, religion and all this, and I thought: "Oh will I?" I hadn't been happy with giving up church that's true … And I changed my mind there and then! I decided: "No, I'll finish." So I told him. Of course I was upset because I thought the world of him … Well I made up my mind that day I walked down the prom … And I knew I wouldn't be married in the Catholic Church; so it would be a Registry Office … Well I wouldn't be happy giving up my religion; it's no good saying I would. I'll tell you what I used to think: "What if I go out, and get knocked down and die?" You know, if I went out I could get knocked down or anything; and if I died sudden what would happen? That was always my fear. That's what made me do it I think. It was more important for me to hold on to my religion. I knew I couldn't be really happy without it. (Bernadette, b. 1915, Co. Mayo)

She named her son after his father, who supported the boy financially, but she did not let him meet him. The father kept in contact by letter and never remarried. Bernadette said that she had lived a celibate life since the birth of her son. Bernadette's experience supports the findings of the previous chapter, that Irish Catholic women largely upheld their religion after emigration, and it vividly illustrates the personal sacrifices that some women were forced to make in order to do so.

Apart from the two unmarried mothers and the one nun, all the other respondents married. The one Protestant woman, a Baptist, married an English Methodist in a Baptist chapel. The majority of the 36 Catholic women who married chose Irish Catholic husbands. Southern Irish Catholics were their most popular choice of marriage partner, with twenty women marrying them. Five women married Northern Irish Catholics and three women married second generation Irish Catholics. Two women married Northern Irish Protestants and six women married English Protestants. When the numbers of Northern, Southern and second generation Irish men are added together it can be seen that 30 were Irish and that 28 of these were Catholic.[5] The minority of Protestant men who married the Catholic women all changed to Catholicism before the marriage and were married in a Catholic church. Marrying a husband of the same religion was reported as being very important to all the women, and all of the Catholic women whose future husbands were Protestants when they met said that they would not have married them if they had not converted because they would not have been able to marry in a Catholic church otherwise.

There is also evidence that parental influence in the choice of marriage partner continued after emigration. Several women who dated English men in Lancashire were persuaded by their parents in Ireland to marry Irish men instead and they all subsequently followed their advice. Bridget became engaged to an English male nurse whilst she was working at a hospital in Kendal. However, her fiance and his parents and sister paid a visit to her family in Cork city whilst Bridget remained working in Kendal and there was a clash of cultures:

> No, they didn't like him at all. I'll tell ye what it was: the wedding was all arranged. Me dad says to him, like a typical Irishman, he says "I tell ye what, we'll go up to the pub and celebrate and have a drink." And his mother said "Neither dad, nor I, nor my son or daughter ever drank, and we're not going to start now!" Well he said for them to go up and have an orange juice but they wouldn't. Anyway, me father wrote to me the next day and he said "For goodness sake don't marry him. Marry an Irishman, you'll have more of a life with him." He said "Any man that don't take a drink is no good." (Bridget, b. 1930, Cork City)

Bridget terminated the relationship and soon after this she met her future husband, a man from Co. Roscommon whom her parents were delighted with. Irish attitudes to drinking obviously varied between families since earlier in this chapter, Patricia was seen to have been told to end a relationship with a boy because his family drank.

Some women did not even consider marrying English men because they knew it would upset their parents. Mary was born in Co. Mayo in 1917 and she followed her sister to London in 1938 to train as a nurse. She enjoyed a successful career and lively social life, dating a succession of English doctors before she decided that it was time to settle down and marry. Although she admitted to always having been attracted to doctors, romance and social class came secondary to nationality and religion in her choice of marriage partner. In 1952, when she was thirty five, she realised that time was running out for her to have children but she would not contemplate marrying any of her previous suitors because her sister had already upset the family by marrying an English doctor. Instead, Mary decided to marry a patient whom she had nursed for less than a week in Preston Royal Infirmary after he had a motor-cycle accident. He was a factory worker, and he was Irish and Catholic:

> Well I nursed him and he was up and about for a few days before he went home. And I went out one afternoon with him and we got talking and he was a nice feller. I was getting on and it was a case of: 'At eighteen you say What's he like? At twenty-five you say What does he do? At thirty you say Where is he?' ... I thought me time was catching up with me ... Well I'd met a lot of Englishmen anyway ... I could ha' been married three or four times to doctors ... I said 'One Protestant is enough in our family!' My father and mother were so upset at that sister o' mine marrying that English Protestant, I couldn't be looking at them at all! (Mary, b. 1917, Co. Mayo)

Most emigrant women ultimately chose their own husbands but within the boundaries of suitability which had been defined by their parents; much the same as they would have done had they remained in Ireland.

There was also one case which showed evidence of emigration even sustaining the traditional Irish marriage system of the economic match. The pattern of marriages being arranged between rural families on an economic basis, with a prospective bride bringing in a dowry commensurate to the size of farm she was marrying into, became widespread in Ireland after the Famine and the practice continued into the twentieth century. Most of the respondents who were born in rural Ireland believed that their parents had experienced matched marriages. The fieldwork which was undertaken by the anthropologists Arensberg and Kimball in West Clare between 1931 and 1934 depicts a life of total subordination for women in a patriarchal rural Irish society. The economic match was the only system of marriage and women were prized for their chastity before, and fecundity after, marriage. [6] Historians have subsequently shown that the traditional patterns Arensberg and Kimball observed had largely only been in place since the Famine and the community which they researched had already begun to experience change and decay at the time of their study. From the late 1930s young Irish women were increasingly choosing emigration rather than the life of subordination which becoming a country wife entailed.[7]

Ironically, one respondent's history showed that emigration could also provide a wider network of matchmaking after the enlightened local supply of prospective brides proved unwilling. Maureen was born in Wigan in 1923. Her mother had been raised in a fiercely sectarian working-class area of Liverpool's docklands and she was a staunch Irish nationalist. Her father was born on a small farm in Co. Mayo and worked in the coal mines in Wigan. Maureen's strongest childhood memories were of a loving home where her parent's songs and stories romanticised Ireland and left her with a desire to go back to the idyllic countryside from which her parents had been exiled. Maureen's mother had been widowed before she met her father. Her first husband was a man from Co. Sligo and she still kept in touch with her first husband's sister after she remarried. Maureen's mother arranged a match with this sister-in-law between Maureen and the woman's widower son, who was fifteen years older than Maureen and had a seven year old daughter. Maureen welcomed the arrangement since it enabled her to live in the Irish countryside she had idealised all her life. The reality of life in rural Ireland did not, however, match her romantic preconceptions. Despite Maureen's Irish Catholic upbringing and her strong sense of Irish identity which had made her want to live in Ireland so much, her English birth and accent marked her as an outsider and she was shunned by a xeno-phobic rural community which exported most of its own people but was not prepared to tolerate immigrants, even one of Irish parentage who had been brought up to consider herself Irish:

> When I came here I was kind of a blow-in. And the people here in this village … they were all married to each other like, and I kinda didn't fit in. And even the mother-in-law, when she was in a bad temper, used to say that she had her eye fixed on another woman, for her son, who had land. So that's why I worked all the harder. To let them know, you know, that I was as good as them. They didn't include me in anything … They'd say I was English … They said English people weren't as good as Irish and I was classed as an Englishwoman. (Maureen, b. 1923, Wigan)

Not alone is there evidence of parental control of marriages conti-nuing after emigration, the traditional Irish practice of matchmaking, which was increasingly losing favour with women in Ireland, can be seen to have at times endured because of emigration.

Apart from the two respondents who had illegitimate children, no other respondent reported having sex before they were married. Caroline had been raised by nuns in a convent, where she had predictably not received any education about sexual matters. Although she had left the convent eight years previously, she said that she was still sexually naive when she married at twenty four:

> Even from the day I got married, I was still as thick as two short planks as far as marriage or having a partner was concerned, because I'd never, ever, you know … alright I'll give to ye straight. I was a virgin when I got married and believe you me, I didn't know anything about the facts

o' life. Honest to God, I just didn't know anything. I walked into marriage thick. (Caroline, b. 1944, Co. Cavan)

The most common impression gained from the respondents is of sexual inhibitions continuing throughout married life in Lancashire. Lena married an Irish Catholic and, in hindsight, she regretted both her own and her husband's sexual inhibitions:

> We were always warned by my mother that if a man touched us: "Take your shoe off and hit him!" ... Even if ye wanted them to make love to ye, ye'd be frightened in case they'd think ye were cheap ... And I think it left an awful stigma because when I got married sex was the most horrible thing I ever had, you know. I think there can be too much warning. I often thought since, that if I had my way over again I would never be a virgin, get married a virgin. That's a fact. I'd have a far broader outlook on love and sex and marriage. I'd make a better wife too I think. Because we didn't give our husbands much really. Honest, we didn't, you know. We were terribly shy, right through 'till my husband died really. (Lena, b. 1930, Co. Galway)

Although Lena blamed her own sexually repressed upbringing for a less than fulfilling marital life, she admitted that her husband was also shy. It has already been shown that Irish boys were often brought up to be as sexually unaware as girls and the fact that most respondents married Irish Catholic men is probably significant to the generally inhibited picture of married sex which most respondents portrayed.

Contraception was an issue which faced many of the women for the first time after emigration. The absence of the ban on information about, and availability of, contraception in Lancashire compared with Southern Ireland theoretically made it at least an option. In practice, however, some women remained unaware about birth control even after emigration. Siobhan was one of the youngest respondents, but she echoed the views of several women who were totally unaware of the existence of any form of contraception before the publicity which surrounded the introduction of the birth control pill in the 1960s. When asked if she had planned her six children she replied:

> Did I hell! No! There was no such thing as the pill then was there? No, I knew nothing. I just went crying to the doctor every time. And he done nothing for me! (Siobhan, b. 1938, Co. Donegal)

Of the women who were aware of contraception, Barbara was the only respondent who said that she successfully limited her family in the full knowledge that she was contravening Catholic Church laws. She had four sons whose births were planned after she picked up information about birth control when she and her new husband emigrated from Donegal to Glasgow in 1956. Adherence to Catholic teaching was the main reason why most women who said that they were aware of contraception did not use it. Some of the women resented and even questioned their Church's ruling but dared not oppose it. Maura was one such woman, who reluctantly felt obliged to follow the instructions of her insensitive priest against the advice of her doctor:

> The only thing the doctor suggested was sterilisation. And I mean that was out o' the question – with ye being a Catholic ... I had five caesarian operations and I remember talking to Fr Turner and he says: "Of course it's nothing nowadays at all isn't that. Not like when I had me appendix out!" Yeah, they used to say: "There was never a mouth sent into the world that there wasn't food sent for." But that isn't true. Because half the world is hungry, isn't it? (Maura, b. 1927, Co. Roscommon)

Some women showed a fatalistic attitude to childbirth and chose to leave their life in the hands of God and the priests rather than take medical advice. After having four children, Maggie was advised by her Catholic doctor to use contraception because she had a weak lung and further childbirth could kill her:

> I wouldn't have no contraceptives or nothing! ... Dr Williams is a Catholic, you know, and he tried to tell me I'd had enough ... He said he could give it to me because I had a weak lung ... No way would I use anything. It didn't make any difference to me if I died having a kid. I just thought, if God wants me he'll take me anyway, won't he? It doesn't matter which way ... I had two more children, and I was in me forties then. I was forty four when I had me last one. (Maggie, b. 1926, Co. Donegal)

Even women who were in the medical profession went against the advice of colleagues in order to follow the rules of their religion. Agnes had been a nursing sister in St Helen's before her marriage and she then had six difficult pregnancies and labours in quick succession. She suffered from life threatening toxaemia each time but after the first three were born in the same maternity hospital she chose different hospitals for her subsequent births, eventually resorting to a private hospital for the last one, because she was embarrassed by the reaction of medical staff:

> Oh Lord, I hated them discussing the fact that I was in having another baby and I was in again with toxaemia, you know ... When I was being discharged every time I was given the same lecture – to go to the birth control centre. If you're following your religion you don't go

to birth control centres. (Agnes, b. 1925, Coventry. Moved back to
Roscommon as a baby, 1926)

Maeve was a doctor whose first baby died after she developed
toxaemia during her pregnancy. She was diagnosed as having chronic
nephritis and advised not to have any more children unless her
kidneys improved. She knew that she was risking her life but she
had two more difficult births and refused to agree to sterilization
because of her religious beliefs:

> There was no such thing as family planning in my day, just the safe
> period, that's about all. I would look on it differently now but being
> brought up in a Catholic country where everything was very rigid, you
> didn't really think about it. I would no more have practised birth control
> than fly because we were brought up to believe it was wrong. The
> consultant wanted to sterilize me because I was very bad with all my
> births. I had toxaemia and had to have a caesarian when I was seven
> months pregnant each time. He said if I had another child, I'd either be
> a permanent invalid or it would kill me ... Yet I wouldn't agree. I would
> agree now, because as you get older you realise that you have to be
> sensible about these things. (Maeve, b. 1917, Co. Tipperary)

With the benefit of hindsight, and the knowledge that most of their
daughters used contraception, most women, at the time of their
interview, shared Maeve's opinion that contraception should not be
barred to Catholics. Agnes and Maggie were still convinced that it
was sinful. Barbara was, however, the only Catholic respondent who
did not believe that contraception was a sin over thirty years ago.

Oral evidence from Elizabeth Roberts' study on working class
women in Barrow, Lancaster and Preston between 1940 and 1970,
suggests that these Irish emigrant women's general attitudes to
contraception were at variance with those of most Lancashire
women. From a total of 98 respondents, only one said that she did
not use any means of planning her family and 'it would appear that
most, indeed almost all, couples planned their families'.[8]

Conclusions

There was a general continuity in the pattern of Irish women's
personal relationships with the opposite sex before and after emigration. Most women remained celibate before marriage. Parental
approval was often still an important consideration in their choice of
husband and parents could still exercise control over their emigrant
daughters' relationships. The majority of women in this study
married Irish Catholic men and many of these did so in order to please

their families. All of the women interviewed married their husbands in their own Church. Most women did not use contraception after marriage, either because they were unaware of it or, more usually, because it contravened Catholic Church regulations. Many women displayed a fatalistic attitude towards childbirth. They believed that the number of children they had, and whether or not they survived childbirth, were matters for God, not themselves, to decide.

Robert Kennedy's claim, which was shown at the beginning of the previous chapter, is worth repeating since it has also been tested in this chapter:

> The most disaffected Irish Catholics were most likely to be found among the Irish abroad than at home. Those who were most willing to go along with the conventional expectations of their church were also the ones more likely to remain in Ireland, to accept the large family ideal of Catholic teaching and to marry early enough in life to turn the ideal into actuality.[9]

The results of the research in this chapter support those found in chapter 5, that Catholicism remained a major influence on Irish women's lives after emigration. The combined results of the two chapters do not support Kennedy's claims. The Irish women in Lancashire, studied here, would not appear to have been 'disaffected Catholics.'

Notes

1. See bibliography for examples, especially: Stephen Humphries, *A Secret World of Sex*, 1988; Diana Gittins' article in, *Oral History*, 1975; Elizabeth Roberts, *A Woman's Place*, 1984; Pat Ayers' article in, *Labour and Love*, 1986.
2. *Commission on Emigration and other Population Problems 1948–1954*, 1956. [Pr2541] p. 357.
3. C.E.O.P.P., para. 211, p. 99.
4. Sean O' Ciarain, *Farewell to Mayo: An emigrant's memoirs of Ireland and Scotland*,1991, p. 88.
5. See appendix, table 7: Husbands of Catholic respondents classified by nationality and religion.
6. Conrad M. Arensberg, *The Irish Countryman*, 1959. First pub. 1937. Conrad M. Arensberg and Solon T. Kimball, *Family and Community in Ireland*, 2nd. ed.,1968.1st. ed. 1940.
7. Terence Brown, *Ireland: A Social and Cultural History 1922–1985*, 1985, pp. 183–188.
8. Elizabeth Roberts, *Women and Families*, 1995, p. 77.
9. Robert E. Kennedy, Jr., *The Irish*, 1973. p. 193.

CHAPTER SIX

National identity

Most women who emigrated from Ireland during the first half of the twentieth century never returned to live in that country permanently. The majority of them emigrated when they were young women and spent more years of their lives living in Britain than in Ireland.[1] This chapter will investigate the effects which emigration had on Irish women's sense of national identity. Evidence from oral testimonies will establish how Irish women's sense of Irish national identity was formed during their years living in Ireland and how strong it was when they left Ireland. Most importantly, the chapter will address the extent to which Irish women's national identity was maintained, transformed or lost after emigration

Women's national identity in post-independence Ireland

The consolidation of a unique Irish national identity was a major preoccupation of the leaders of the new state and they were keen to emphasise a distinction between the new Irish nation and its former colonizer. Irish identity was, therefore, marked as Gaelic and Catholic, as opposed to English and Protestant. The Gaelic revival had started at the end of the nineteenth century and it had been an important element in nationalist ideology during the struggle to obtain independence from Britain. After partition the 'rediscovery' of a unique Irish cultural identity was vigorously continued by the Irish state and Gaelic sports, music, dancing and language were actively promoted.

During this period of early Irish independence, most of the respondents were going to school in Ireland. From the time of the formation of the Free State the education department followed a policy which was aimed at instilling a Gaelic culture into the children of the nation, and the national schools were targeted as the ideal place in which to foster a new Gaelic nation. In 1922, Padraig O'Brolchainn, the new chief executive officer for education, spoke of the direction which Irish education was to follow for the next fifty years:

> In the administration of Irish education, it is the intention of the new government to work with all its might for the strengthening of the national fibre by giving the language, history, music and tradition of Ireland, their natural place in the life of Irish schools.[2]

One of the respondents, Eileen, provided text books which she had kept from her schooldays. These were shown to other respondents and many women recognized them and reported that they had read them when they were at school. A glimpse at the pages of these books shows how contemporary school textbooks faithfully followed the romanticised promotion of all things Irish. The preface of *The Voice of Ireland Reader*, which was aimed at older national schoolchildren, began with the sentence:

> The aim of this book is "the strengthening of the national fibre" by interesting the pupils of our National Schools in the antiquities, agriculture, industry, trade and commerce of their own land.[3]

It would appear that the most successful means of promoting a nationalist version of Irish history to schoolchildren was through song. The songs contained in *Ballads of Irish History for Schools*,[4] which was widely read by schoolchildren in the new Irish state, were well known to most of the respondents and the ballads were remembered long after their schooldays. Many of these ballads had been written by the leaders of 'Young Ireland' for publication in *The Nation* in the mid-nineteenth century and they were still being widely promoted in Irish schools a century later:

19. Children holding pikes in commemoration of the 1798 Irish rebellion, Co. Wexford, 1938. Reproduced courtesy of Mary Walsh.

> At school we always used to sing all these patriotic songs, like all about Ireland ... we sang 'The West's Awake' and all these songs, you know, in school: "Sing oh hurray, let England quake, we'll fight till death for Ireland's sake." Did you ever hear that song 'The West's Awake'? And 'Father Murphy'? ['Boolavogue'] (Molly, b. 1931, Co. Longford)

The revival of the Irish language was a major part of the official state policy of the Gaelicisation of Irish schools but it was less successful than intended

20. A Camogie team, Co. Wexford, 1945. Camogie, the female equivalent of the men's game of hurling, was promoted in girls' schools after independence. Reproduced courtesy of Mary Walsh.

and was not so popularly received by pupils as was the singing of patriotic ballads in the English language. Oral evidence shows that the extent to which the Irish language was used in schools varied widely and it was dependent upon the expertise and enthusiasm of individual teachers, especially in the smallest national schools. Many women recalled the Irish translation of their name being used in school and most of them recited prayers, poems and songs in Irish at school, and spoke of prizes being awarded for this. Only one woman, Maeve, spoke Irish regularly at home and this can be attributed to her unique family circumstances. Her father was the Secretary of Education in the Irish Free State, a personal friend of Eamon de Valera, and a leader of the programme for Gaelicising Ireland.

Ironically, teachers in the ever-decreasing Protestant national schools possibly felt more obliged to rigidly follow the instructions of the education minister regarding the Irish language than did those in Catholic schools. Lily's schooldays in Athlone were made miserable because of her insecure schoolmaster's crusade to instil Irish in his pupils, to such an extent that she left school illiterate in the English language:

> We had a horrible master. He was the most hateful man; he hated us anyway! He was terrible, he was really hard on us. Under the law you were compelled to learn Gaelic you see. Yes in our school! And, to prove to the authorities we were doing as the law said, he was a tyrant when he was teaching this. You couldn't speak a word of English, you had to address him in Irish the whole time. He was a tyrant for that; he was

worse than the Catholics themselves! ... I never got to read or write English very well until after I left school. But I got really good at the Gaelic. (Lily, b. 1929, Athlone)

The irony of the situation was not lost to Lily; when she described her master as being 'worse than the Catholics themselves' she was reflecting the fact that Protestants such as she were being indoctrinated with the ideals of Gaelic Catholic Ireland. Their comparatively small numbers often resulted in the mixing of all denominations of Protestants in the Church of Ireland National schools and they consequently lacked the unified religious atmosphere which was present in Catholic schools. In Lily's case, Sunday school was the place where she received her Baptist religious instruction, not national school where she felt alienated from the Church of Ireland culture. The divisive denominational differences within Protestant national schools such as Lily's, coupled with the ever-present threat that they might be closed down if numbers fell any further, resulted in a more secular education which placed more emphasis on adhering to the official policy of Gaelicisation. Lily's national school was Protestant in the sense that it was not Catholic but Protestant religious doctrine came second to Irish in its curricular emphasis.

The situation was much different in Catholic national schools such as this one, attended by Marion, where the Irish language was accommodated, so long as it did not interfere with the main purpose of Catholic education:

> If you knew your Catechism you were alright. That's how I sum up the Irish schools and the Irish way o' life ... Because where I was brought up they didn't give two hoots whether you knew anything else; but you had to know about that ... I mean the only Irish that we ever learned over there was our prayers – the Our Father and the Hail Mary [she recites these two prayers in Irish]. The only thing we learned in Gaelic was our prayers. That was it, it didn't go any further. As long as we knew our prayers. I think they would have taught us them in Japanese if they could! (Marion, b. 1932, Co. Mayo)

At the time of partition the majority Catholic Church effectively controlled the education system in Southern Ireland and its power was unchallenged by the new state: Irish education remained state-funded but Church-controlled.[5] Through its control of the Catholic schools, the Catholic Church hierarchy ensured that their schoolchildren were left in no doubt about their national identity; they were Catholic Irish first and Gaelic Irish second.

Lily's recollections of living in Ireland portray a constant picture of her being denied an Irish identity because she was Protestant.

Most civic and national ceremonies were undertaken in the presence of Catholic Church dignitaries and Lily remembered that the minority of Protestant citizens were excluded from joining in any of these events:

> All our friends were Catholics, all our neighbours were Catholics. It was just the odd times things would come up. There were certain things that you would understand as their national ways. Like if there was a parade on St Patrick's Day, or if there was anything that was a national happening, you would know that you weren't welcome there. You know, your place wouldn't be there. It was just a thing that happened automatic. They would understand that you wouldn't attend, and you'd understand that you couldn't attend. It was never spoken about much but that's the way it was. (Lily, b. 1929, Athlone)

It is clear that Protestants were increasingly being marginalised in Southern Ireland; to such an extent that they were being denied an Irish identity.

21. Pupils at St Louis Convent School, Kiltimagh, graduating as 'Children of Mary', 1946. Reproduced courtesy of Josephine Haran.

Women were also being marginalised in Irish society at this time but they were not denied an Irish identity, as the Protestants were. Instead, their national identity was being changed, and separated from that of Irish men. Things had started well for women in Southern Ireland after independence. In 1922 the Free State government granted the vote to all women over 21, six years before Great Britain granted equal voting rights to women.[6] Six female deputies were elected to the first Dail but by 1952, thirty years after partition,

there were even fewer women in electoral politics than in 1922 as women's role in political and public life diminished in the twenty-six counties. Successive governments pursued policies which increasingly restricted women's involvement in the public sphere. The 1927 Juries Act, for example, virtually excluded women from jury service by making it necessary for them to formally apply. The Conditions of Employment Bill of 1935 regulated the hours of women workers and the industries which were allowed to employ them. A particularly strong attitude against married women working was evident. A marriage bar existed in the public sector until 1973 and between 1926 and 1966, only about 5% of Irish married women were registered as employed.[7] The new Constitution of Ireland in 1937 placed the family at the core of Irish society and prohibited the introduction of any legislation on divorce. Most significantly for women, it located their ideal position as caring for the family within the home. Article 41:2 stated that:

2.1   In particular, the State recognizes that by her life within the home, woman gives to the State a support without which the common good cannot be achieved.

2.2   The State shall, therefore, endeavour to ensure that mothers shall not be obliged by economic necessity to engage in labour to the neglect of their duties in the home.

Thus by 1937 the ideal of Irish woman in the family home was being equated with patriotism, necessary for the 'common good' of the State. The personification of Irish womanhood which was most idealised in popular culture was that of the devout Catholic mother. Irish girls and women were immersed in a culture which idealised Ireland as a Gaelic Catholic homeland where their duty lay in service to the family and to the Church.

Alongside Catholicism and family duty, the other important element of Irish national identity was that it was anti-English and this had a significant effect on the lives of the respondents at the time of emigration because they were going to live in England. Maura, who emigrated at the age of eighteen to work as a chambermaid in Morecambe, remembered only ever hearing bad things said about England in her schooldays:

In a sense we were taught to hate. We were taught this history, you were sorta taught to hate England and then sent here. What do you know when you're eighteen? ... They used to say that they don't go to church, and this and that. (Maura, b. 1927, Co. Roscommon)

Several of the respondents reported that they particularly associated England with being a pagan country before they emigrated:

Because in Ireland they'd say when you were coming to England: "Oh watch yourself, you'll lose your religion!" They did. They thought it was terrible, you know; coming to this pagan country. (Molly, b. 1931, Co. Longford)

Not only were young emigrant women made to feel guilty about leaving their homeland, they could also be instilled with a morbid fear of England before they left.

Irish National Identity after Emigration

There is evidence that young Irish women in England often felt a strong sense of fear just after they emigrated, and that this was generated more by their negative preconceptions about England than their actual experiences. Rosie emigrated from Dublin with her husband in 1952. On their first night in Lancaster they went to a local pub with relatives. She recalled how she thought that a group of Australian soldiers were Black and Tans, and that the drink she ordered was poisoned:

That night they took us down to the Midland, and I saw all these soldiers in … They were Australian soldiers, you know, but I thought they were Black and Tans. And then I asked for an orange. At home you used to get a bottle of orange but they just gave me undiluted orange. I thought they were trying to poison me. And then the soldiers being in there, that just finished it, and I got home … to tell the truth, I don't think I trusted them when I came over here, d' you know what I mean? (Rosie, b. 1926, Dublin)

The recollections of Joan, who left Co. Mayo for domestic service in Sidcup, Kent in 1933, show that the warnings against fraternising with males, that were impressed upon young women in Ireland, could be given an even more sinister resonance when applied to males in England:

We were warned before I left home about the South American er? … ye'd get an injection and ye'd land up in South America in the white slavery. Oh it was common knowledge … I remember once, I wanted to see a picture and I went in in the daytime, in Sidcup, to see it. And them cinemas used to be very dark. And there was only one [*vacant*] seat down the side, and the girl put me into it. I couldn't see who it was that was next to me but oh, I wasn't long sitting down there when I heard it was a man next to me. I thought, "Oh, a white slaver! This injection is coming any time!" I had sense enough to get up, and I went back until I got another seat. I think I kicked out at him or something. I nearly died. (Joan, b. 1915, Co. Mayo)

The fear of English society, which many women brought with them, was fortunately lessened by their actual experiences as they spent some time in England. These two quotes from Molly show that she was frightened to even look at a Protestant church when she was growing up in Longford and she was pleasantly surprised at the benign nature of Protestant worship that she encountered in Lancaster:

> On our way to Mass on a Sunday there was a big, big Protestant church on our left, and I used to say to me brothers and sisters, "Don't look at the church!" I always remember, we were frightened to look at a Protestant church in case it'd be a sin on our souls or something.

> I saw a lot of Salvation Army; which we didn't see in Ireland. They used to march up and down Dale Street on a Sunday morning. I used to think they were lovely actually, 'cause I mean, they used to play lovely music an' everything. And I thought, well they're not doing any harm to anybody ... I was sort o' thinking, well there's only one God and there's good and bad everywhere. (Molly, b. 1931, Co. Longford)

For Molly, along with several other respondents, emigration sig-nalled a more enlightened attitude towards Protestants. It is significant though, that Molly also said in her life history that she would not have contemplated marrying a non-Catholic; she married a man from Donegal. The Catholic respondents generally displayed a belief that Catholicism was spiritually superior to Protestantism. Whilst Protestants appear to have been accepted by most respondents as suitable friends and colleagues, there is evidence that they were not so keen to accept them into their families. Most respondents married Catholic men and the minority of women whose prospective husbands were Protestants would not have married them unless they converted to Catholicism first. The main reason for this was the Catholic Church's strong disapproval of mixed marriages at this time. When Olivia's brother was married in a Protestant church in Birmingham, she asked her parish priest in Lancaster whether she and her other brother should attend the service:

> He was getting married in a non-Catholic church, and so I saw the priest from St Peter's, and I explained to him ... and he said: "Go to the church by all means but don't take part in the service" ... And my other brother had been over from Dublin and he went up the wall: "What do you think my mam would have thought of it!" ... And we went to the wedding but, I mean, it was my youngest brother and me not able to take any part ... and I started crying and I couldn't stop. I cried my eyes out at that wedding ... You know, I couldn't understand it [the service]. It's the first one I'd ever been to, and I saw the difference. (Olivia, b. 1930, Dublin)

Olivia cited part of the reason for her being so miserable at her brother's wedding was that it was different to the Catholic weddings she had been accustomed to. The years covered here are prior to the general reforms in the Catholic Church after the Second Vatican Council. Masses were still being conducted in Latin and this particularly marked the difference between Catholic and Protestant services. Most women also commented that they found a big difference between funerals in Ireland and England, and between Irish and English funerals in England. They all agreed that they preferred to attend Irish funerals and many remarked that they found English funerals to be 'cold':

> The first funeral I went to here, I'll never forget it. My next door neighbour got pneumonia and his wife invited me to the funeral. Well it's a much colder affair here in this country; there's not the same closeness of people. But the first time I went into this crematorium, and I saw those curtains closing, I thought: my God! I was getting really upset, and not a lot upsets me … I've gone to real Irish wakes over here though. The majority of funerals that I've gone to over here are Irish people I suppose. The thing is, at home you meet all your friends and relations at funerals and then they all go to the pub. The men used to go to the pub; the women join them now but they usen't to years ago. I know a lot of English people don't agree about that drinking but I think it's good. I really do. I want a good Irish funeral and I want loads o' whiskey at it. I want them to play 'Tabhair dom labh' – 'Give me your hand'. I don't mind who sings it but I wouldn't mind the Wolfe Tones. (Eileen, b. 1927, Co. Wexford)

Eileen's quote shows that funerals performed a major social function for emigrants in that they provided a venue where: 'you meet all your friends and relations'. Most of the respondents reported that Irish funerals were generally widely attended and they also cited many instances of Irish people who had died in England being 'taken home' for burial. Funerals of Irish people, either at home or in England, enabled families and communities which had been scattered by emigration to come together again.

Overall, the respondents generally portrayed in their life histories a consciousness of being different from their neighbours in Lancashire. This was often noted in small ways such as in this example from Olivia:

> When we come out of the baby clinic on Thurnham Street, me and this other woman used to go in this cafe for a cup of tea … Well, unconscious to myself, I used to always make the sign of the cross after I'd finished eating. Until one day, when she said to me: "Why do you keep doing

that?" ... but even now, I still bless myself when I'm passing a church. (Olivia, b. 1930, Dublin)

Olivia tried to modify her Catholic habit of blessing herself after this incident. Accent was a mark of distinction which could not be so easily hidden, and women were not generally keen to lose their accents in any case. Many respondents expressed having some difficulties in communication when they first emigrated, not only because of the difference in accents but also the different names for some things:

> My God, I couldn't understand her and she couldn't understand me; this woman in the shop, she was really Lancashire ... and one day I went in and I asked for two pans [loaves]. And she said: "What sort of pans, what are you cooking in them?" (Rosie, b. 1926, Dublin)

> I was very conscious of my Irish accent, very conscious of it. But then, having said that, I wasn't going to try an English accent either. I didn't want to lose my Irish accent and I hope I haven't done. (Eileen, b. 1927, Co. Wexford)

Many women appear to have had problems with both understanding and being understood by English people in their early years of living in England. All of the respondents have retained their Irish accents and most women expressed pride that they had done so. The fact that they wanted to retain their accent is significant because it is just one indication of the main reason why the respondents generally reported feelings of being different from their Lancashire neighbours: they were different in many ways because they *wanted* to be so.

Many women said that they preferred the company of Irish friends, although this was not always easy in towns with a small Irish population. Eileen lived in three places in England: Cleethorpes, Liverpool and Heysham. Of the three, she preferred her time living in Liverpool because:

> I was more at home in Liverpool because there was an Irish community there ... It was quite easy to go across to Dublin and get home as well. (Eileen, b. 1927, Co. Wexford)

All of the respondents made English as well as Irish friends but many commented that their closest and longest friendships were with Irish women. Many close friendships had started when they met other Irish mothers when they took their children to Catholic schools and Irish dancing and music classes. Lancaster did not have a large Irish community but Irish dancing classes in St Peter's Catholic school provided a meeting place for Irish mothers:

> Through the children's school, through Irish dancing, that's how I got to know people. The people I got to know when my children were small are the people I know today. I have two very close friends since then. Through the Irish dancing I got to know a lot of people. (Rosie, b. 1926, Dublin)

Sunday Mass was also cited as the place where many women first encountered friends in Lancashire.

Several respondents said that they had noted differences between Irish, English and Scottish people, and there was a general consensus that the English were more aloof than the Scots and Irish:

> I come down here from Glasgow, and I thought in them days the Scottish people were more like Irish, you know. I thought yous were were all so posh down here when I come down … I always thought English people were posher. And when I came down, I thought, God, I'm not going to fit in here, I'm too rough! (Barbara, b. 1935, Co. Donegal)

> English people are not as friendly, you know, as Irish or Scotch people. Oh yeah, they think they're all bloody royalty, most do. They're snobs like, most of them.'Cause I was down at that church for God knows how long before one would say hello to ye. They probably thought you were a gypsy, maybe … I don't dislike the English or anything because, you know, I think they're well-mannered and all the rest of it, but there's that little bit of stand-offishness, you know; they don't want you to get close. (Oonagh, b. 1936, Co. Donegal)

Irish emigrants can be seen to have formulated their own stereotypes of personalities based on nationality and some respondents experienced racism from people in Lancashire, which was based on commonly circulated, negative stereotypes of the Irish.[8] Eileen's previous description of Irish wakes indicated that English people considered the Irish to be heavy drinkers but this was largely a stereotype which related to Irish men. Irish women were more likely to be affected by the jokes which portayed the Irish as stupid, and by the view that the Irish had too many children:

> This English woman said to me: "Irish people are all the same, they do nothing but have loads o' children!" And I didn't agree with her certainly and I had a run-in with her. (Rita, b. 1930, Co. Wexford)

Although negative experiences with English people certainly played their part in Irish women tending not to have been assimilated into the Lancashire community, there is more evidence from the oral histories that Irish women chose to keep themselves separate. This woman, Marion, echoed the reflections of the majority of the respondents when she said that she had both English and Irish friends, but that her Irish friendships were on a deeper level:

> Oh yes, you'd be more comfortable with Irish people. Because the majority of them were Catholics, and even if they weren't Catholics they knew your views, you were all on the same level. Again, having said that, I know quite a number of English people, and I find that I can get on with them, but then there would be a different side to that sort of friendship, because they wouldn't know about our Irish culture and stuff and wouldn't understand half of it. (Marion, b. 1932, Co. Mayo)

This sense of being different from English people was widespread within the sample of respondents.

The colonial relationship between Britain and Ireland (which had only ended for Southern Ireland either during the lifetime of the women in this study or in their parents' lifetime) was a major barrier to assimilation for many respondents.

> I didn't say a lot, I listened. It took me a long time to see that they [*the English*] were just people the same as everybody else. Not that I'm political minded but ... I was conscious of the wars that Ireland had to fight to get independence. Oh yes, I was conscious of that. I would not say anything out of place, that an English person might pick me up on and make me cross. Because it didn't suit me to be cross about the political situation in Ireland because I had to live over here! You just have to go along with the people and do the best you can, and you just have to keep quiet. (Eileen, b. 1927, Co. Wexford)

Eileen's comment that 'you just have to keep quiet' shows that she was reluctant to assert her Irish nationalist opinions amongst people in Lancashire. She also prefaced her views by saying 'not that I'm political minded' which was significant because it suggested that she felt it necessary to qualify having Irish nationalist political beliefs. This was common amongst the respondents and can be attributed to the more recent renewal of conflict in Northern Ireland since 1969. It is apparent that the Troubles caused many Irish people in Britain to refrain from Irish cultural activities and keep a low profile. Before many women spoke about anything which indicated their having Irish Republican sympathies, they were keen to point out that they were talking about the Official I.R.A. and not the Provisional I.R.A. of more recent times. The recent Troubles caused most of them to be initially reticent about disclosing their political views during the years of this study but sensitive questioning usually resulted in them being forthcoming. When women did speak about their political beliefs prior to 1960, they mainly exhibited strong Irish nationalist sympathies. Many of them recounted stories of atrocities which were committed by the Black and Tans in Ireland. Two of the older respondents gave first hand accounts of encountering the Black and Tans:

> I can still see the Black and Tans. They used to come and search our home and pull us all out o' bed. I can still see them. They knew we had brothers, even though they were away in England. They were searching our house for me brothers. That same week – that we were all searched in our village – there was three shot in the village. And in the school, we used to be pulled out and stood along the wall by the English soldiers. And the poor old souls, when they used to go in for their pension, they used to shout "Halt!" at them on the bridge going into Aclare. And of course they didn't hear them and they'd shoot them dead on the street. There was five shot dead the day my grandmother was buried. I remember it so well because we were worried about my mother and father who had gone to the funeral ... We were longing for my mother and father to come and make sure they didn't get shot on the road. (Attracta, b. 1911, Co. Sligo)

More women recounted stories that had been told to them by their parents and these all described atrocities perpetrated by the Black and Tans in Ireland. It is difficult to discern whether the stories had been elaborated but their main significance lies in the fact that the women themselves believed them to be true and they provided a reason not just for emigrant women to be afraid of English people, but to have an antipathy towards them.

Respondents were also asked if they could remember any particular songs which they had sung or heard after they emigrated. Although a few popular songs from musicals of the time were mentioned, Irish songs predominated in their recollections and they fell mainly in to two types: rebel songs, including many of those they had sung at school plus more recent ones like 'Kevin Barry'; and songs about emigration, which usually referred to emigrants as exiles and romanticised Ireland. The first verse of just one song, which several respondents mentioned, 'The boys from the County Mayo', is typical of the content of songs about emigration:

> Far away from the land of the shamrock and heather
> In search of a living as exiles we roam
> But whenever we chance to assemble together
> We sing of the land where we once had a home
> Those homes are destroyed and our soils confiscated
> The hand of the tyrant brought plunder and woe
> The fires are now quenched and our hearths desolated
> In our once happy homes in the County Mayo.

Their continuous revival in emigrant ballads ensured that accounts of England's past tyrannies in Ireland remained long-lived in popular memory. Alun Howkins has found that 'the words of songs collected from ordinary people can tell the historian something about these people's attitudes, ideas and feelings'.[9] The songs about rebellion and emigration which Irish women sang in Lancashire were yet another part of their emigrant culture which glorified their homeland and denigrated their present residence.

A desire to transmit an Irish identity to their children was shown in chapter three to have been one reason why Irish emigrant women often spent the summer holidays in Ireland. Many of the women were also keen to involve their children in Irish cultural activities in Lancashire:

> I took the children to Irish dancing. They know quite a bit about Ireland, and also they had Irish music in the house. As they grew older we'd go out to St Patrick's Club, and we'd come back a little merry, and we'd put on the Irish music and the rebel songs'd be played. The girls were supposed to be in bed but they were down listening to this music. (Eileen, b. 1927, Co. Wexford)

Since Irish cultural activities often took place in Catholic churches and schools it is not surprising that Lily, the sole Protestant respondent, did not take part in them. She did, however, make friends with both Irish and English people after she emigrated. She reported that she considered herself to be Irish and never tried to lose her accent but she was annoyed by the fact that people in Lancashire automatically assumed that because she was Irish, she was Catholic.

One Catholic woman also reported that, like Lily, she felt that her Irish identity was not as valid as some peoples. Caroline grew up in a convent and has little knowledge of her family background. She emigrated to Lancaster and married an Irishman. Her accent is Irish, she was a champion set dancer and she taught Irish dancing at a Catholic Club in Lancaster. She plays Irish music on the accordion and has frequented Irish clubs since moving to Lancashire. Yet she still has problems with her Irish identity because she can not identify with a family in Ireland:

> I wouldn't let anybody run Ireland down or nothing like that but Ireland to me doesn't mean as much as probably it would to you and people that were brought up in a family environment, you know ... That's what I missed most, not having a sort of home to go to: roots. Now I didn't have any roots in Ireland, only Nazareth House, and you wouldn't call them roots really would you? A lot of them say they want to go back to

their roots but I've no roots to go back to. And I do miss that you know. I do ... I mean you wouldn't really call me Irish, would ye? ... You know, the real Irish would talk about their family homes, and what it was like, and always wanting to go back. I mean, I have no such home to talk about. The only home I've got to talk about was the Nazareth House and, to me, we probably missed out on a lot o' the real Ireland ... Honest to God, I think it must be lovely to come from a big ould Irish family! (Caroline, b. 1944, Co. Cavan)

Lily's frustrations at being wrongly identified as an Irish Catholic and Caroline's reflections that she was not one of the 'real Irish' once again highlight the importance of the influences of family and Catholicism on Irish national identity. The majority of the respondents, however, fitted into Caroline's 'real Irish' category: they were Catholic and they had families in Ireland. Apart from Lily and Caroline most women in this sample had no problems with their national identity in Lancashire: they were Irish emigrant women who lived in England.

It is particularly ironic that although Irish women generally retained a very strong allegiance to their original family and community in Ireland, that allegiance does not always appear to have been reciprocated. Several women recalled that emigrants were sometimes resented by family members who stayed at home because of family obligations:

My youngest brother, he resents the fact that he was the one that had to stay at home. He got away for a few years before my father died but he had to go back then ... he's a wee bit bitter and envious of us. He thinks we've had a wonderful life. (Rita, b. 1930, Co. Wexford)

Other women indicated that they would have been happy to go back to Ireland to live but that they were unsure how their English husbands would be received:

I can't see us going back for good. Albert would love to go back, he'd go back anyday because there's a great fuss made of Albert. But I think he's treated as a visitor and I don't know how he would be treated if we were back there permanently. (Annie, b. 1929, Co. Cavan)

Another respondent's husband was certain that he would not be accepted into her homeplace. Elsie was born in Wexford and her husband Tom was born in Scotland. Elsie's recollection is followed by that of her husband Tom:

Perhaps if I hadn't met Tom I might have gone back home. Who knows how life would have gone on? But this is our destiny isn't it? ... They'd definitely accept me in the village because all the people there are the people I went to school with. (Elsie, b. 1931, Co. Wexford)

Well I love going to Ireland but I would never go there to stay. And do you know why? Well all you have to do is listen to the people in the pubs. You're an incomer or a blow-in. You're quite acceptable as a holidaymaker, and they love you and everything else, but the minute you put down some roots – you're a blow in. (Tom, b. 1932, Edinburgh)

The consensus of the respondents seemed to be that although they had tried hard to maintain an Irish identity in England, they were conscious of not wholly belonging to English or Irish society. Annie's reflections are typical of those of many of the emigrant women:

I never wanted to break me ties with there ... As the years went on I became, you know, more attached to Ireland, and the rural area, and my upbringing and everything ... I'm not too sure where I belong actually at times ... I suppose you never get away from your roots but I suppose I'm a bit different from people who never left there ... I can see things in a broader sense. (Annie, b. 1929, Co. Cavan)

Annie's phrase, 'A bit different from people who never left there', is a perfect description of the Irish identity of emigrant women in Lancashire.

Notes

1. See chapter 2, for general information on Irish women's ages at emigration and emigrants' destinations. The more specific information on the sample of respondents, also given in chapter 2, shows that they too largely conformed to this pattern.
2. Quoted in John Coolahan, *Irish Education*, p. 41.
3. *The Voice of Ireland Readers: Calling to the Men and Women of To-morrow: Senior Book*, undated but contains the owner's handwritten date of 1939.
4. *Ballads of Irish History For Schools, fourteenth edition*, dated by the owner, 17th Feb. 1940.
5. See Tom Inglis, *Moral Monopoly*, 1987, especially pp. 53–58, for the growth and extent of Catholic Church control of education.
6. The emancipation of women in the United Kingdom in 1918 had been restricted to women over 30 and it was not until 1928 that legislation in Great Britain reduced the female voting age to 21, followed in Northern Ireland in 1929.
7. Robert E. Kennedy, *The Irish*, 1973, p. 159.
8. See Liz Curtis, *Nothing but the same old story: The roots of anti-Irish*

racism, 1984, for the history and extent of negative stereotypes of the Irish.

9. Alan Howkins, 'The Voice of the People: the social meaning and context of country song' *Oral History*, vol. 3, no. 1, 1975, p. 50.

CHAPTER SEVEN

Reflections

In providing not only much needed information about a group of people who have been hidden in the historical record but also involving them in setting up the research agenda, this study has transformed the understanding of a key theme in Irish and British social history. Irish emigration to Britain has been substantial in the twentieth century but little is known about these emigrants' lives apart from where they settled and the jobs they were employed in. Even when these aspects of Irish emigration have been studied, the majority group of Irish emigrants – women, have been largely unacknowledged. Until now, the personal effects which emigration had on people's lives, and particularly their relationships with the families they left behind, have not been regarded as significant issues in the study of Irish emigration. This study has shown them to have been most important areas of Irish emigrant women's lives.

Oral history was deliberately employed as the main research method in order to identify and address various issues from the perspective of emigrant women themselves and the main themes of this book evolved from the priority which they were accorded in the life-histories of the interviewees in this sample. Throughout every life-history in the sample two themes overwhelmingly emerged as having been major influences on Irish emigrant women's lives: religion and the family. Family and religious influences shaped Irish women's lives both before and after emigration.

Most women emigrated for economic and some for social reasons, but whether the initial impetus for emigration was economic or social, obligations to the family most often outweighed individual choice in women's reasons for leaving home. Sparing their family from the necessity of keeping them and leaving in order to send money home to educate younger siblings were common motives for emigration. The position in the family was significant here, with older sisters in poorer families often leaving school earlier than their younger brothers and sisters who then had the benefit of furthering their education from the proceeds of the money which emigrants sent home. Sparing their families from shame was also a major reason why single pregnant women emigrated and they were often assisted by female relatives. The most convincing evidence of women emigrating in order to fulfil family obligations was shown in the examples of women who complied with their family's expectations by emigrating against their own wishes.

Within this study, family networks were also the most important means of arranging and maintaining emigration but only in the area of concealing a pregnancy was the network gendered. In other instances women were as likely to have their emigration arranged by, or to go and stay with, male relatives. Most women who left Ireland went to live in British towns where they had relatives.

Significant contact was maintained between Irish women in Lancashire and their families in Ireland. Letters and parcels were frequently sent from both sides of the Irish Sea. Ireland was the favourite, and in most cases the only, holiday destination of emigrants and, significantly, most women referred to these visits as 'going home'. Life-cycle stages affected the frequency of visits to Ireland, especially motherhood. Some women went back to Ireland to give birth. Ironically, for many women motherhood brought an additional incentive of wanting to acquaint their children with their Irish families and cultural inheritance but this was often accompanied by increased financial restraints which made their visits to Ireland less frequent. Female emigrants often took on the responsibility of caring for family members in Ireland and they were more likely to return home for this reason than were Irish men. The death of parents and siblings in Ireland often brought about a change in the pattern of visits.

Religion, especially Catholicism has also been shown to have strongly influenced Irish women's lives both before and after emigration. Irish Catholic women generally kept up their religious practices in Lancashire, for social as well as spiritual reasons. It was, however, in the area of personal relationships that religion would appear to have had most influence on emigrants lives. The one Baptist woman in this study married a Methodist man and all the Catholic women who married either married Catholic men, usually Irish, or ensured that their husbands-to-be converted to Catholicism before marriage. All the married women in this sample married in churches of their own denomination. Family expectation was given as a major reason for marrying within their faith. All the women who became mothers also had their children christened in their own religion. The two unmarried mothers lived celibate lives after the births of their children and expressed a belief that they had committed a mortal sin. Although most respondents expressed a widespread level of ignorance concerning sexual matters, Catholic Church teaching was the main reason why most women did not avail of contraception. A fatalistic attitude towards pregnancy and childbirth was most apparent and some women consciously chose to risk their lives rather than their souls.

One explanation for the strength of continuity of traditional religious behaviour and family ties amongst Irish women in Lancashire between 1922 and 1960 can be found in the investigation of national identity. All but two emigrants in the study reported that they felt distinctly Irish and had not assimilated into British society. Of the two women who had problems with their national identity; one was Protestant, and the other was not brought up in a family home in Ireland. The other respondents were all raised in Irish Catholic families. The newly-independent Ireland which the women left was distinctly post-colonial. Irish identity was strongly promoted and an important measure of Irishness was its distinction from anything English. A woman's perception of Irishness was increasingly associated with her religion, and with her role within the family and the home. The cultural climate of newly-independent Ireland generally ensured that emigrants going to England left with a desire to uphold their Irish identity in the country from which Ireland had only recently gained independence; as an Irish woman's identity was defined by her Catholicism and her role within the family she was less likely to sever these ties after emigration than to adopt strategies of maintaining them from a distance.

The strong familial, cultural and religious ties which emigrant women in Lancashire maintained with Ireland challenges the accepted notion of the assimilation of Irish women in 20th century Britain. In a pioneering oral study of Irish women in Britain, Mary Lennon observed that 'women face greater pressures to adapt to British society than men because of their family role and responsibilities'.[1] The argument of this book is that in the forty years following independence Irish women faced more pressures to avoid assimilation precisely because 'their family role and responsibilities' were affected by post-colonialism. Whilst Irish women's comparative invisibility in Britain has been taken to mean that they asserted their Irishness less readily than Irish men, their absence from the male-dominated Irish public spheres of pubs, clubs and associations could also be evidence of a continuance of Irish patriarchal culture after emigration. Irish emigrant women were maintaining their Irish identities within their families and by their extensive links with their family homes in Ireland, and their devotion to the Catholic Church, they were transmitting an Irish cultural identity to their children.

Notes

1. Mary Lennon *et al.*, *Across the Water*, 1988, pp. 15–16.

22. Carrying on the tradition. Second-generation Irish dancers pictured at St Patrick's School, Heysham, 1975. Reproduced courtesy of Mary Walsh.

Appendix of Tables

Table 1: Population of Ireland, 1841–1961
(Thousands)

Year	Ireland	Southern	Northern
1841	8,175	6,529	1,646
1851	6,552	5,112	1,440
1861	5,799	4,402	1,397
1871	5,412	4,053	1,359
1881	5,175	3,870	1,305
1891	4,705	3,469	1,236
1901	4,459	3,222	1,237
1911	4,390	3,140	1,250
1926	4,229	2,972	1,257
1936	4,248	2,968	1,280 [a]
1951	4,332	2,961	1,371
1961	4,240	2,815	1,425

Note: a. 1937
Source: This table is reproduced from J. A. Jackson, *The Irish in Britain*, 1963, p. 25.

Table 2: Birthplace of respondents

Irish county of birth	Total born in that county
Cavan	2
Clare	1
Cork	1
Donegal	8
Dublin	5
Galway	1
Kerry	1
Leitrim	1

Irish county of birth	Total born in that county
Longford	1
Mayo	6
Roscommon	5
Sligo	1
Tipperary	1
Westmeath	1
Wexford	3
English town of birth	Total born in that town
Coventry	1
Wigan	1

Table 3: Average annual net emigration from Southern Ireland classified by gender, 1871–1971

Period	Males	Females	Females per 1,000 Males
1871–81	24,958	25,214	1,010
1881–91	29,257	30,476	1,042
1891–1901	20,315	19,327	951
1901–11	11,764	14,390	1,223
1911–26	13,934	13,068	938
1926–36	7,255	9,420	1,298
1936–46	11,258	7,453	662
1946–51	10,309	14,075	1,365
1951–56	21,657	17,696	871
1956–61	21,915	20,486	935
1961–66	7,523	8,598	1,143
1966–71	4,950	5,831	1,178

Note: Figures for the years 1871 to 1951 are extracted from C.E.P.P., Table 13, p. 23; and the figures for 1951 to 1971 are taken from a table compiled by Bronwen Walter in R. King (ed.), *Contemporary Irish Migration*, 1991, p. 12.

Table 4: Year of emigration of respondents

Year	No. of respondents who emigrated that year	Year	No. of respondents who emigrated that year
1910	2	1947	3
1928	1	1948	1
1933	1	1949	2
1935	1	1950	6
1936	1	1951	3
1938	1	1952	2
1939	1	1953	1
1942	1	1955	1
1943	1	1956	2
1944	1	1960	1
1945	3	1961	1
1946	1	1965	1

Table 5: Age of respondents on initial emigration
from Ireland

Age at emigration	Total emigrants of this age	Age at emigration	Total emigrants of this age
1	1	17	1
2	1	18	7
3	0	19	6
4	0	20	6
5	0	21	5
6	0	22	0
7	0	23	5
8	0	24	2
9	0	25	0
10	0	26	2
11	0	27	0
12	0	28	0
13	0	29	0
14	0	30	0
15	1	31	0
16	1	32	1

Table 6: Migration patterns of respondents

Name	Places lived in from birth to the mid-1960s
Agnes	Coventry; Roscommon; Rochdale; Nottingham; Stockport; Manchester; St Helen's; Roscommon.
Alice	Dublin; Liverpool; Dublin; Liverpool; Morecambe.
Annie	Cavan; Navan, Co. Meath; Ashton-under-Lyne; Morecambe.
Attracta	Sligo; Chicago, U.S.A.; Sligo; London; Morecambe.
Barbara	Donegal; Glasgow; Lancaster.
Bernadette	Mayo; Manchester; Blackpool; Kendal; Lancaster.
Breda	Roscommon; London; Morecambe.
Bridget	Cork; Kendal; Bradford; Lancaster.
Caroline	Cavan; Belfast; Navan, Co. Meath; Lancaster.
Claire	Clare; Belfast; Halifax; Morecambe.
Dearbhla	Donegal; Derry; Preston; Lancaster; Morecambe.
Dolores	Donegal; Preston.
Eileen	Wexford; Cork; Dublin; Cleethorpes; Liverpool; Wexford; Heysham.
Elsie	Wexford; Warwick; Larne, N.I.; Accrington.
Joan	Mayo; Sidcup, Kent; Bromley, Kent; Preston.
Kathleen	Leitrim; Sligo town; London; Preston; Blackpool; Preston.
Katrina	Roscommon; Longford; Bangor, N.I.; Blackpool; Blackburn; Clitheroe; Blackpool; Morecambe.
Sr Kevin	Kerry; London; Lancaster.
Kitty	Mayo; Accrington.
Lena	Galway; London; Margate, Kent; Morecambe.
Lily	Athlone; Lancaster; Morecambe.
Maeve	Tipperary; Dublin; Keighley, Yorks.; Liverpool.
Maggie	Donegal; Derry; Cork; Baton Rouge, U.S.A.; Donegal; Morecambe.
Marion	Mayo; Dublin; Preston.
Mary	Mayo; Brentwood, Essex; London; Preston.
Maura	Roscommon; London; Lincoln; Morecambe; Manchester; Morecambe.
Maureen	Wigan; Sligo.
Molly	Longford; Dublin; Lancaster.
Noreen	Donegal; Lancaster.
Olivia	Dublin; Preston; Lancaster.

Name	Places lived in from birth to the mid-1960s
Oonagh	Donegal; Manchester; Lancaster.
Patricia	Donegal; Derry; Manchester.
Philomena	Mayo; London; Preston.
Rita	Wexford; Liverpool; Heysham.
Rosie	Dublin; Lancaster.
Sarah	Dublin; Liverpool; Dublin; Liverpool; Plymouth; Liverpool; Heysham.
Sheila	Dublin; Liverpool; Lancaster; Dublin; Lancaster.
Sinead	Roscommon; Manchester; Preston.
Siobhan	Donegal; Milnthorpe; Lancaster.
Theresa	Roscommon: Southport; Dewsbury; Blackpool; Grange-over-Sands; Preston

Table 7: Husbands of Catholic respondents classified by Nationality and Religion

Nationality & Religion of Husband	No. of Respondents who Married
English Catholic	0
English Protestant	6
Southern Irish Catholic	20
Southern Irish Protestant	0
Northern Irish Catholic	5
Northern Irish Protestant	2
Second generation Irish Catholic	3

Biographies of Oral History Respondents

The following measures have been adopted in order to preserve confidentiality:

1. Respondents are identified only by first name pseudonyms.
2. Names of family members and friends have also been changed.
3. Places of birth are given at large town or county level.

Agnes

b. 1925, Coventry. R.C.

Father: farmer and seasonal migrant. Mother: housewife.

7 children in family, she was the eldest.

Moved back to Co. Roscommon with her parents aged about 1 year.

Her father died when she was 10. Left national school aged 16. Worked on the farm and in the home. Emigrated with her sister in 1945, aged 20, to train as a nurse in Rochdale. She met her Irish Catholic husband, who was a neighbour of her parents, whilst she was home on holiday. She moved to Nottingham after she qualified as a nurse and he was a seasonal migrant in Lincs. She joined the same nursing agency as her sister and worked in Stockport and Manchester. Her husband-to-be was now working in the coalmine in St Helen's. She found a job in a hospital there and they married when they were both 27. She had 7 children. 6 were born in St Helen's and 1 after they moved back to her husband's farm in Co. Roscommon.

Alice (Sister of Sarah)

b. 1910, Dublin. R.C.

Father: tailor. Mother: housewife who was a lady's companion before marriage.

6 children in family, she was the youngest. The family emigrated to Liverpool in 1910 when she was less than a year old. She returned to Dublin for a few years in her childhood and then went back to

Liverpool. Left school at 14 and worked in a sewing factory. Married English husband in August, 1939 after a ten year courtship. Her husband left to serve as a soldier in the Middle East when war broke out in September and they did not live together again until 1944. Three children, the first was born in 1945 when she was 35.

Attracta

b. 1911, Co. Sligo. R.C.

Parents: farmers

8 children in family. All emigrated to U.S.A. or England. Left school at 13, worked in the home and on the farm. Emigrated to her brother in Chicago in 1928, aged 17. Worked as a domestic servant and a nurse. She loved life in Chicago and became an American citizen. Returned home on holiday in 1938, for the first time in ten years. Her mother was taken ill and she was persuaded by her family to stay nearer home and not go back to America. She had left a fiance in Chicago. She went to London just after the War started in 1939. Worked in an hotel but she contracted diphtheria and spent six months in hospital. In 1940 she came to a brother in Morecambe to convalesce as London was being blitzed. She got a job cleaning railway carriages. Married an Irish Catholic friend of her brother's. 5 children.

Annie

b. 1929, Co. Cavan. R.C.

Parents: farmers

10 children in family. Left school at 14 and went to work as a housekeeper for 2 local bachelor farmers. Left after 10 months when an aunt, home from America, offered to pay for her to attend technical school. Went as a boarder to a college run by nuns in Co. Meath for 2 years. Emigrated in 1949, aged 19 to train as a nurse in Ashton-under-Lyne. Met her husband (English Prot.) and moved to Morecambe. She did not tell her family in Ireland he was Protestant. He converted to Catholicism before he met them. 3 children.

Barbara

b. 1935, Co. Donegal. R.C.

Father: labourer. Mother: housewife.

9 children in family. Left school at 14 and worked for the next two

years looking after the children in a local household. From 16–21 she looked after the children in a doctor's house. Married a local man in 1956. Emigrated to Glasgow soon after the marriage. Moved to Lancaster and moved in with husband's mother, who had by now left Donegal. 4 children. Barbara and her husband were divorced in 1985.

Bernadette

b. 1915, Co. Mayo. R.C.

Father: policeman then a farmer when his brother died. Mother: dressmaker.

6 children in family. All emigrated except 1 brother who stayed on the farm.

Left school at 13. Helped her mother at home. Emigrated to Manchester 1939, to her cousin. Worked in a shop. Moved to Blackpool with her cousin. Became pregnant in Blackpool. Her boyfriend was a divorced Protestant and she would not marry him after a priest told her it would be a mortal sin. Her priest sent her to the Catholic Rescue Society and she gave birth to her son in 1945, in a home for unmarried mothers run by nuns. The Society arranged for her to work as a housekeeper to two Catholic spinster sisters in Lancaster. She went there with her baby son and stayed for forty years. She did not marry.

Breda

b. 1928, Co. Roscommon. R.C.

Father: farmer. Mother: housewife.

8 children in family. Left school at 14 and worked at home. Emigrated to London in 1947 after a cousin came home on holiday and organised a job for her in domestic service. She worked there for 9 months and left after she secured a job as a chambermaid in Morecambe which she had seen advertised. Married in Morecambe (S.I. Cath.). Did not work outside the home after marriage. 6 children.

Bridget

b. 1930, Cork city. R.C.

Father: confectioner. Mother: housewife

4 children in family. She was the only one to emigrate. Left school at 14 and went to work with her father and brother in a confectionery factory. Went to a friend in Kendal and worked as a receptionist in a hospital. Met her Irish Catholic husband and moved with him to

his sister in Bradford. She married and trained as a nurse in Bradford. Moved to Lancaster, again to follow his sister. Her husband worked away a lot in the construction industry. She worked part-time as a nurse after marriage. 2 children.

Caroline

b. 1944, Co. Cavan. R.C.

No knowledge of father and little of mother. She was placed in a convent at the age of two and remained there until she was 16. Her mother visited her sometimes but would never speak about her family. She only discovered that she had a brother living in the neighbouring boys' home when she was told by a nun at the age of 11. She was never allowed to see much of him. When she left the convent she went to work as a ward maid in Belfast but was sacked and placed in another convent for striking a staff nurse who called her a bastard. She ran away, back to her original convent. Went to look after priests in a seminary in Co. Meath. She became engaged to a local farmer but ran away before the wedding. A friend from her convent days arranged a job in Lancaster, where she met and married her Irish Catholic husband. 2 children.

Claire

b. 1932, Co. Clare. R.C.

Parents: farmers.

She was the eldest of 7 children. Left school at 13. Went to Belfast, lived with an aunt and worked as a chambermaid in an hotel. Emigrated to Halifax aged 18 after her mother sent her to live with an aunt when she found out she had been dating a Protestant in Belfast. Worked as a chambermaid and waitress. Met and married her Irish Catholic husband in Halifax. Her sister and brother emigrated to her in Halifax. Moved to Morecambe when her husband found work there. 2 children.

Dearbhla

b. 1926, Co. Donegal. R.C.

Father: farmer. Mother: housewife.

8 children in family. Left convent boarding school at 16 and went to work for an aunt in Preston in 1942. Her aunt had a boarding house and she stayed there for over two years. Moved to a friend

in Lancaster. Worked in a cafe in Lancaster and then moved to nearby Morecambe and worked a hotel there. Met her husband in Morecambe (N.I. Prot.). He converted to Catholicism. 6 children.

Dolores

b. 1932, Co. Donegal. R.C.

Father: farmer. Mother: housewife.

4 children in the family. Went to national and technical school and left at 17. Worked at home until she emigrated in 1951, aged 19. She went to where her friend was already working in an hotel in Preston. She worked as a chambermaid. She married a Northern Irish Catholic. 5 children.

Eileen

b. 1927, Co. Wexford. R.C.

Father: blacksmith Mother: housewife.

4 children in family. Left school at 17 after attending national and vocational school. Worked in shops in Cork and Dublin. Met her Irish Catholic husband whilst at home on holiday. They married in Wexford when she was 32 and emigrated after the honeymoon. He was already working in England. They moved with his job to Cleethorpes, Liverpool and finally Heysham. 2 children.

Elsie

b. 1931, Co. Wexford. R.C.

Father: farm labourer. Mother: housewife.

6 girls in the family. She was the youngest. 1 sister died aged 20, the rest all emigrated to England. Left school at 14. First paid job was when she was 17. Domestic servant for 2 years. Emigrated in 1951 aged 20. Went to live with her married sister in Warwick and trained as a nurse. Met her husband (2nd gen. Irish. R.C.) Married in Wexford. Lived in Larne N.I. where her husband's parents lived. Moved to Accrington with his job. 5 children.

Joan

b. 1915, Co. Mayo. R.C.

Father and mother: farmers.

12 children in family. All emigrated to America or England. 2 returned. Left school at 14 and worked on the farm. Emigrated to
Sidcup, Kent in 1933. Went to where 2 of her brothers and 1 sister
were living. Worked as a domestic servant. During the War she was
moved to Bromley and then Preston to work in munitions factories.
Met her Irish Catholic husband in Preston at the end of the War.
She worked as a waitress after marriage but left after her 2nd son
was born because she could not afford the nursery fees. 4 children
but 1 died.

Kathleen

b. 1921, Co. Letrim. R.C.

Father: farmer who died when she was 9. Mother: farmer.

She was the youngest of 6 children. All emigrated, eldest brother to
America and rest to England. She stayed on at national school until
she was 16 because her mother got an extra half crown per week on
her widow's pension whilst she was at school. Went to work at Sligo
mental hospital and emigrated to train as a nurse in 1944, aged 23.
Went to London but transferred to a hospital in Preston to be nearer
her sister, who was living in Blackpool. Met and married an English
man in Preston and had 2 children. The marriage broke up when
she was pregnant with her 2nd child. He divorced her and married
again. She has never remarried because of Catholic beliefs. She
progressed to the position of matron and raised her children alone.

Katrina

b. 1925, Co. Roscommon. R.C.

Father: farmer. Mother: housewife.

3 children in family. Went to national school and then convent
boarding school. Left aged 17. Went to live with an uncle, who was
a policeman, and his family in Bangor, Co. Down. Worked in an
aircraft factory in Newtonards. Managed to obtain resident's permit
through her uncle's connections but when they would not renew it,
she emigrated to Blackpool in 1947. Worked as a waitress. Moved to
another waitressing job in Blackburn, then worked in another hotel
in Clitheroe. She was promoted and went to work in the office of

an hotel in Blackpool. Moved to Morecambe to manage the office in a larger hotel. Met and married her English husband in 1959. No children.

Sr Kevin

b. 1924, Co. Kerry. R.C.

Father: farmer. Mother: housewife.

4 children in family. She was the only one to emigrate. Left school at 14 and worked on the family farm. She wanted to emigrate and become a nun in 1944 but was not given a permit to enter Britain. After the War ended in 1945, she emigrated to London aged 21 with three first cousins and they all entered the Ursulines. She worked in the convent kitchens for most of her life. Moved to Lancaster with the order.

Kitty

b. 1943, Co. Mayo. R.C.

Father: farmer. Mother: housewife.

6 children in family. Left school at 14 and worked on family farm for 5 years. Emigrated in 1961. Went to Accrington to live with an aunt after she had attended a family wedding there. Worked in Woolworths. Met her Irish Catholic husband at a Pioneer meeting in Accrington. Two children.

Lena

b. 1930, Co. Galway. R.C.

Parents: farmers.

9 children in family, she was the 5th. Left school at 14. Worked on family farm. Emigrated aged 15 in 1946. Went to London to work as a domestic servant. Left after 3 months. Went to live with a sister and had 9 jobs in 4 months. Went to another sister in Margate. Trained as a psychiatric nurse. Moved to Morecambe with a friend to work as children's nurses at Middleton Holiday Camp. Met and married her husband (N.I. Cath.) Worked part time as a nurse after marriage. 4 children, 2 miscarriages.

Lily

b. 1929, Athlone, Co. Westmeath. Baptist.

Father: Wool buyer in a woollen mill. Mother: housewife.

She was the second of four girls. Attended Protestant national school. Left at 14 unable to read and write properly in English because her schoolmaster had concentrated on Irish. She was a shop assistant in Athlone. Emigrated to Lancaster in 1950 to nurse at the infirmary but hated it and left after a few months to live with her uncle in nearby Morecambe. Her uncle found her seasonal work in a cafe and when that finished she went to live with an aunt who found her work in a shop. Married her English Methodist husband in Morecambe in 1953. 4 children.

Maeve

b. 1917, Co. Tipperary. R.C.

Father: college lecturer, school inspector and Secretary of Education. Mother: housewife.

5 children, she was the only girl. 4 of the 5 emigrated. The family moved to Dublin when her father was transferred there. She attended boarding convents in Monaghan and Dublin and she went on to Dublin University where she graduated with a degree in medicine. Two of her brothers also became doctors and two were lawyers. She emigrated with a friend in 1944 and they both worked in a hospital in Keighley. She met her husband (Liverpool Irish) in Keighley. She moved to Liverpool to be near him. They married and she worked in general practice whilst her husband went to medical school. When he qualified, she worked part-time. He became a consultant psychiatrist. 3 children. She lost one baby.

Maggie

b. 1926, Co. Donegal. R.C.

Father: farm labourer. Mother: domestic servant before marriage, housewife after marriage.

Eldest of 13 children. Left school at 14 after receiving two years of secondary education which was paid for by two of her aunts. Worked in a factory in Derry. In 1949 she entered a convent in Cork and emigrated to Baton Rouge, Louisiana in 1949 as a novice missionary nun. She left the order and returned to Donegal because of ill health. She went back to work in Derry but when her work permit was not renewed she went to work as a chambermaid in Morecambe. Married an English Methodist who converted to Catholicism. 6 children.

Marion

b. 1932, Co. Mayo. R.C.

Father: farmer. Mother: housewife.

9 children in family. Left school at 14. Worked on the farm and then moved to Dublin and into domestic service. Went back to Mayo after two years in Dublin but could not find work and emigrated to Preston aged 20. Her brother and his wife were already living in the town. She worked in Woolworth's until her marriage to an Irish Catholic. 5 children.

Mary

b. 1917, Co. Mayo. R.C.

Father: farmer. Mother: housewife.

13 children in family. Attended national school until she was 12 and then convent school. Left school aged nearly 18. Worked on family farm and emigrated in 1938 to train as a nurse in Brentwood, Essex. Her sister was already nursing there. Moved to a hospital in London during the War and then on hospital ships. Went to the Normandy landings and to India. After the War moved to work in a hospital in Preston to be near her sister who was married in Blackpool. Met her husband (N.I. Cath) when he was a patient in her ward. They married 6 months later, when she was 36. 3 children.

Maura

b. 1927, Co. Roscommon. R.C.

Father: farmer. Mother: housewife.

6 children in family. Left school at 14 and worked on the family farm until emigrating to London in 1945, aged 18. Worked as a domestic servant. Went to live with her sister in Lincoln. Moved to Manchester and then went to Morecambe after seeing a job for a chambermaid advertised. Met and married an Irish Catholic. He was a labourer and they eventually bought a boarding house. 6 children.

All her brothers and sisters emigrated. 2 brothers to England. 3 sisters to San Francisco. 1 sister to Lincoln and then she moved back to Roscommon.

Maureen

b. 1923, Wigan. R.C.

Father: from Mayo, coalminer. Mother: Liverpool Irish, housewife.

8 children in family. (4 were from her mother's first marriage to another Irish miner who was killed). Left school at 14. Worked in a sewing factory until she was called up for war work. Worked in Oldham making lorries. Saved up during the war to go to Ireland and she went there for the first time in 1945 for a holiday with her father's family. She returned every year and a marriage was arranged by her mother and her mother's former sister-in-law. She married this sister-in-law's widowed son in 1951 and moved in to the small farm in Co. Sligo with him, his mother and his daughter. 7 children

Molly

b. 1931, Co. Longford. R.C.

Father: gamekeeper. Mother: housewife.

13 children. Went to national school and then technical school. Left at 17. Went to Dublin and worked as a domestic help, looking after children. Emigrated to her sister in Lancaster in 1951, aged 20.

Started nurse training but met her Irish Catholic husband and left nursing after 12 months to get married. 7 children, 1 died in infancy.

Noreen

b. 1913, Co. Donegal. R.C.

Parents: farmers.

11 children in the family. She married a local farmer. Emigrated to Lancaster in 1936, aged 23 with 3 children to join her husband. He had been a seasonal migrant, coming to Sedbergh each year. He got a permanent job in Lancaster as a railway labourer and she came over. She had 8 children, one died in infancy. Worked part-time throughout marriage.

Olivia

b. 1930, Dublin. R.C.

Father: brewery worker. Mother: housewife.

5 children in family. Left school at 14. Worked in a mill with her sister. When she was made redundant she emigrated to Manchester

in 1950. She had a brother and cousins living there. Worked in a factory and decided to move to Lancaster after visiting her married sister there. Worked in a factory in Lancaster. Met and married her husband (S.I. Cath.) Did not work outside the home after marriage. 4 children.

Oonagh

b. 1936, Co. Donegal. R.C.

Father: county council labourer. Mother: housewife.

6 children in family. Left school at 14 and worked at home for a year then in domestic service. Emigrated in 1955 with a cousin. The cousin had a sister and two brothers in Manchester. Worked in a cafe in Manchester. Met and married her husband there (S.I. Cath.). He was a labourer and they moved to Lancaster because of his job. 5 children. She worked as a part-time cleaner after marriage.

Patricia

b. 1925, Co. Donegal. R.C.

Father: rural postman. Mother: died when she was 4. Her father remarried 2 years later and her stepmother was a dressmaker.

9 children in family (7 born to her mother and 2 to her stepmother). Left school at 14. Sewed shirts with her stepmother then went to work in a shirt factory in Derry with her sister aged 18. Emigrated to Manchester with her sister in 1949. Stayed with a cousin. Worked in a shirt factory. Met and married her Irish Catholic husband. Kept a boarding house after marriage. 5 surviving children, 2 stillborn babies and 2 miscarriages.

Philomena

b. 1917, Co. Mayo. R.C.

Father and mother: farmers.

7 children in family. 2 more died in infancy. Left school at 13. Worked on the farm. Emigrated to London in 1935. Worked in domestic service. Two sisters were already there doing the same and two brothers also worked in London. Met her future husband (S.I. Cath) in London. He moved to Preston and they married and lived in Preston. She worked as a ward maid in a hospital and he was a labourer. 5 children.

Rita

b. 1930, Co. Wexford. R.C.

Father: fisherman. Mother: housewife.

5 children in family. Went to national and vocational school and left at 16. Worked in a shop until she emigrated in 1953. She followed her boyfriend, a Wexford man, who was working in Liverpool. She worked in a shop in Liverpool and they moved to Heysham when he got a job there soon after they married. She did not work outside the home after marriage. 3 children.

Rosie

b. 1926, Dublin. R.C.

Father: a fitter in a factory. Mother: worked in a fruit shop before marriage, housewife after marriage.

9 children in family. 4 died in childhood. Her father died when she was a child. Left school at 14. Worked in a firelighter factory and then a sausage factory. She married in 1951 and her husband lost his job soon after. Emigrated with her husband and baby daughter in 1952 to his sister's house in Lancaster. 3 children.

Sarah (Sister of Alice)

b. 1908, Dublin. R.C.

Father: tailor. Mother: lady's companion before marriage and house-wife after marriage.

6 children in family. Her parents emigrated in 1910 when she was 2. She went back to Dublin for a few years in her childhood and then returned to Liverpool. Left school aged 14. Worked in factories in Liverpool and Plymouth. Married an English Protestant merchant seaman in Plymouth in 1932. Moved to Liverpool and then Heysham with his job. 4 children.

Sheila

b. 1923, Dublin. R.C.

Father: farm labourer. Mother: housewife.

The eldest of 8 children. Grew up on a farm on the outskirts of Dublin. Left school at 14 and worked in a cotton mill in Harold's Cross. Left the mill to look after her mother who died when she was 19. Looked after her brothers and sisters whilst her father worked in England. When he came back, she emigrated to Liverpool in 1947. Worked in a stocking factory in Kirkby for a few months and then went to Lancaster to nurse her uncle's dying wife and look after their 4 children. Uncle was a merchant seaman. Went back to Dublin for a while to nurse her dying father. Became pregnant and had an illegitimate son. She went back to her uncle's house in Lancaster, with her son, and raised his children. She never married.

Sinead

b. 1929, Co. Roscommon. R.C.

Father: farmer. Mother: housewife.

5 children in family. Left school at 17 after attending national and vocational school. Worked in the home and emigrated with a cousin in 1950. Went to Manchester to train as a nurse. Met her husband in Manchester (N.I. Catholic). She moved to a hospital in Preston. They were married in Preston and he moved there to work in a factory. She worked part-time after marriage. 4 children.

Siobhan

b. 1938, Co. Donegal. R.C.

Father: county council labourer. Mother: housewife.

The eldest of ten children. She left national school at 13. She was too young to get a job in a factory which she would have liked so she worked as a maid in a dentist's house in the local town for a year and then she was hired as a live-in farm servant. She served three six-month hirings. From the ages of 16–18 she worked as a ward maid in Letterkenny hospital. She then applied for a job in an hotel in Milnthorpe that was advertised in an Irish newspaper and emigrated, along with her cousin in 1956. She was courting her husband to be in Donegal at the time of her emigration. He was Irish and R.C. He emigrated to Lancaster (where he had a sister) soon after her. She moved from Milnthorpe to Lancaster and they married in 1959. He was a labourer. 5 children. She worked part-time in various factory and cleaning jobs after marriage.

Theresa

b. 1928, Co. Roscommon. R.C.

Father: farmer. Mother: housewife.

3 girls in the family. Went to national school and then technical school in Roscommon. Left at 18. Emigrated in 1948 to join her sister as a nurse in Southport. Met her husband (N.I. Prot.) in Southport. He was a teacher. After marriage they moved with his job to Dewsbury, Blackpool, Grange-over-Sands and Preston. 3 children.

Bibliography

Arensberg, Conrad M., *The Irish Countryman: An Anthropological Study*, Reprinted Gloucester, Massachusetts: Peter Smith, 1959. (first pub. 1937)

Arensberg, Conrad M. and Kimball, Solon T. *Family and Community in Ireland*, 2nd edn, Cambridge, Massachusetts: Harvard University Press, 1968. (1st edn 1940).

Arnstein, Walter L., 'The Murphy riots: A Victorian dilemma', *Victorian Studies*, Sept. 1975, pp. 51–71.

Bourke, Joanna, *Husbandry to Housewifery: Women, Economic Change and Housework in Ireland, 1890–1914*, Oxford: Clarendon Press, 1993.

Bourke, Joanna, *Working-Class cultures in Britain 1890–1960*, London and New York: Routledge, 1994.

Brody, Hugh, *Inishkillane: Change and Decline in the West of Ireland*, Harmondsworth, Middx: Pelican Books, 1973.

Brown, Terence, *Ireland: A Social and Cultural History 1922–1985*, London: Fontana Press, 1985.

Bunreacht na h'Eireann (Constitution of Ireland) 1937

Coolahan, John, *Irish Education: Its History and Structure*, Dublin: Institute of Public Administration, 1981.

Curtin, Chris, Jackson, Pauline and O' Connor, Barbara (eds), *Gender in Irish Society*, Galway: Galway University Press, 1987.

Curtis, Liz, *Nothing but the same old story: The roots of anti-Irish racism*, London: Information on Ireland, 1984.

Daly, Mary E., 'Women in the Irish Workforce from Pre-Industrial to Modern Times', *Saothar*, Vol. 7, 1981, pp. 74–82.

Daly, Mary, E., 'Women in the Irish Free State, 1922–39: The Interaction Between Economics and Ideology', *Journal of Women's History*, Winter/Spring 1995, pp. 99–116.

Davis, Graham, 'Little Irelands', in Roger Swift and Sheridan Gilley (eds), *The Irish in Britain 1815–1939*, London: Pinter Publishers Ltd, 1989, pp. 104–133

Diner, H. R., *Erin's Daughters in America: Immigrant Women in the Nineteenth Century*, Baltimore: John Hopkin's University Press, 1983.

Dowling, Michele, '"The Ireland that I would have", De Valera and the creation of an Irish national image', *History Ireland*, Vol. 5, No. 2, Summer 1997, pp. 37–41.

Drudy, P. J. (ed.), *Irish Studies 5: Ireland and Britain since 1922*, Cambridge: Cambridge University, 1986.

Drudy, P. J., 'Migration between Ireland and Britain since Independence', in P. J. Drudy (ed.), *Irish Studies 5: Ireland and Britain since 1922*, Cambridge, 1986, pp. 107–123.

Fahey, Paddy, *The Irish in London*, London: Centerprise, 1992.

Fielding, Steven, *Class and Ethnicity: Irish Catholics in England, 1880–1939*, Buckingham: Open University Press, 1993.

Foster, R. F., *Modern Ireland 1600–1972*, London: Penguin Books, 1989 (first published 1988).

Fox, Robin, *The Tory Islanders*, Cambridge, 1978.

Gibbon, P., 'Arensberg and Kimball revisited', *Economy and Society*, ii, 1973, pp. 479–98.

Glynn, Sean, 'Irish Immigration to Britain, 1911–1951: Patterns and Policy', *Irish Economic and Social History*, VIII, 1981, pp. 50–69.

Hartigan, Maureen and Hickman, Mary J. (eds), *The History of the Irish in Britain: A Bibliography*, London: Irish In Britain History Centre, 1986.

Hickman, Mary J., *Religion, Class and Identity: The State, the Catholic Church and the Education of the Irish in Britain*, Aldershot: Avebury, 1995.

Humphries, Stephen, *A Secret World of Sex: Forbidden Fruit, the British Experience*, London: Sidgwick and Jackson Ltd, 1988.

Hoppen, K. Theodore, *Ireland Since 1800: Conflict & Conformity*, Harlow: Longman Group U.K. Ltd, 1989.

Howkins, Alan, 'The Voice of the People: the social meaning and context of country song', *Oral History*, vol. 3, no. 1, 1975, p. 50.

Hutton, Sean and Stewart, Paul (eds), *Ireland's Histories*, London and New York: Routledge, 1991.

Inglis, Tom, *Moral Monopoly: The Catholic Church in Modern Irish Society*, Dublin: Gill and Macmillan Ltd, 1987.

Jackson, John Archer, *The Irish in Britain*, London: Routledge and Kegan Paul, 1963.

Jackson, John A,.'The Irish in Britain', in P. J. Drudy (ed.), *Irish Studies 5: Ireland and Britain since 1922*, Cambridge, 1986.

Johnson, J. H., 'The distribution of Irish emigration in the decades before the Great Famine', *Irish Geography*, 21, 1988, pp. 78–87.

Kelly, J. M., *The Irish Constitution*, Dublin: University College, 1980.

Kennedy, Liam, *The Modern Industrialization of Ireland 1940–1988*, Dublin, 1989.

Kennedy, Robert E., *The Irish: Emigration, Marriage, and Fertility*, Berkeley and Los Angeles, California: University of California Press, 1973.

King, R. (ed.), *Contemporary Irish Migration: Geographical Society of Ireland Special Publications, no. 6*, Dublin, 1991.

Lee, J. J., 'Women and the Church since the Famine', in Margaret MacCurtain and Donncha O'Corrain (eds), *Women in Irish Society*, Dublin, 1978, pp. 37–45.

Lee, J. J., *Ireland 1912–1985: Politics and Society*, Cambridge: Cambridge University Press, 1989.

Lees, Lynn Hollen, *Exiles of Erin: Irish Migrants in Victorian London*, New York, 1979.

Lennon, Mary, McAdam, Marie and O'Brien, Joanne, *Across the Water: Irish Women's Lives in Britain*, London: Virago Press Ltd, 1988.

Lewis, Jane (ed.), *Labour and Love*, Oxford: Basil Blackwell Ltd, 1986.

Lummis, Trevor, *Listening to History: The authenticity of oral evidence*. London: Hutchinson, 1987.

MacCurtain, Margaret and O'Corrain, Donncha (eds), *Women in Irish Society: the historical dimension*, Dublin: Arlen House, 1978.

MacCurtain, Margaret, 'Late in the Field: Catholic Sisters in Twentieth-Century Ireland and the New Religious History', *Journal of Women's History*, Winter/Spring 1995, pp. 49–63.

McAdam, Marie, 'Hidden from History: Women's Experience in Emigration', *Irish Reporter*, No. 13, 1994, pp. 12–13.

McCullagh, Ciaran, 'A Tie That Blinds: Family and Ideology in Ireland', *The Economic and Social Review*, vol. 22, no. 3, April 1991, pp. 199–211.

Neal, Frank, 'The Birkenhead Garibaldi riots of 1862', *Historic Society of Lancashire and Cheshire*, vol. 131, 1981, pp. 87–111.

Neal, Frank, 'Manchester Origins of the English Orange Order', *Manchester Region History Review*, vol. iv, no. 2, 1990–91, pp. 12–24

Neal, Frank, 'English-Irish Conflict in the North West of England: Economics, Racism, Anti-Catholicism or Simple Xenophobia?', *North West Labour History*, no. 16, 1991/92, pp. 14–25.

Nolan, Janet A., *Ourselves Alone: Women's Emigration from Ireland 1885–1920*. Lexington, Kentucky: University Press of Kentucky, 1989.

O'Carroll, Ide, *Models for Movers: Irish Women's Emigration to America*. Dublin: Attic Press, 1990.

O'Ciarain, Sean, *Farewell to Mayo: An Emigrant's Memoirs of Ireland and Scotland*, Dublin: Brookside, 1991.

O'Connor, Kevin, *The Irish in Britain*, London: Sidgwick & Jackson, 1972.

O'Dowd, Liam, 'Church, State and Women: The Aftermath of Partition', in Chris Curtin *et al.* (eds), *Gender in Irish Society*, Galway 1987, pp. 3–35.

O'Dowd, Mary and Wichert, Sabine (eds), *Chattel, Servant or Citizen: Women's Status in Church, State and Society*, Belfast: Queen's University, 1995.

O'Hara, Patricia, 'What Became of Them? West of Ireland Women in the Labour Force', in Chris Curtin *et al.* (eds), *Gender in Irish Society*, Galway 1987, pp. 70–86.

O'Lochlainn, Colm, *The Complete Irish Street Ballads*, London: Pan Books Ltd, 1984.

O'Sullivan, Patrick (ed.), *The Irish World Wide. Volume 1: Patterns of Migration*, Leicester, London and New York: Leicester University Press, 1992.

O'Sullivan, Patrick (ed.), *The Irish World Wide. Volume 2: The Irish in the New Communities*, Leicester, London and New York: Leicester University Press, 1992.

O'Sullivan, Patrick (ed.), *The Irish World Wide. Volume 3: The Creative Migrant*, Leicester, London and New York: Leicester University Press, 1994.

O'Sullivan, Patrick (ed.), *The Irish World Wide. Volume 4: Irish Women and Irish Migration*, London and New York: Leicester University Press, 1995.

O'Tuathaigh, M. A. G., 'The Irish in nineteenth-century Britain: Problems of integration', *Transactions of the Royal Historical Society*, vol. 31, 1981, pp. 149–173.

Pooley, Colin, 'Segregation or Integration? The Residential Experience of the Irish in mid-Victorian Britain', in Roger Swift and Sheridan Gilley (eds), *The Irish in Britain 1815–1939*, London: Pinter Publishers Ltd, 1989, pp. 60–83.

Redlich, Patricia, 'Women and the Family', in MacCurtain and O' Corrain (eds), *Women in Irish Society*, 1978, pp. 82–91.

Report of the Commission on Emigration and other Population Problems 1948–1954, Pr. 2541, 1956.

Rhodes, Rita, M., *Women and the Family in Post-Famine Ireland: Status and Opportunity in a Patriarchal Society*, New York and London: Garland Publishing, 1992.

Roberts, Elizabeth, *A Woman's Place: An Oral History of Working-Class Women 1890–1940*, Oxford: Blackwell Publishers, 1984.

Roberts, Elizabeth, 'Women's Strategies 1890–1940' in Jane Lewis (ed.), *Labour and Love*, 1986, pp. 223–248.

Roberts, Elizabeth, *Women and Families: An Oral History, 1940–1970*, Oxford: Blackwell Publishers, 1995.

Rossiter, Ann, 'Bringing the Margins into the Centre: A Review of Aspects of Irish Women's Emigration', in Sean Hutton and Paul Stewart (eds), *Ireland's Histories*, London and New York: Routledge, 1991, pp. 223–242.

Rossiter, Ann, 'Bringing the Margins into the Centre: A Review of Aspects of Irish Women's Emigration from a British Perspective', in Ailbhe Smyth (ed.), *Irish Women's Studies Reader*, Dublin, 1993, pp. 177–202.

Rudd, Joy, 'Invisible Exports: The Emigration of Irish Women this Century', *Women's Studies Int. Forum*, vol. 11, no. 4, 1988, pp. 307–311.

Scheper-Hughes, Nancy, *Saints, Scholars and Schizophrenics: Mental Illness in Rural Ireland*, Berkeley: University of California Press, 1979.

Snell, Bradley, *Geographical Distribution of the Irish-Born Population in England 1961*, unpublished M.A. dissertation, Lancaster University, 1996.

Stelfox, Margaret, *The Family, Women and Health: A Study of Health Strategies in Manchester c. 1919–1939*, unpublished Ph.D. thesis, Lancaster University, 1995.

Swift, Roger and Gilley, Sheridan (eds), *The Irish in Britain 1815–1939*, London: Pinter Publishers Ltd, 1989.

Thompson, Paul, 'Problems of Method in Oral History', *Oral History*, no. 4, 1973, pp. 1–55.

Thompson, Paul, *The Edwardians*, Weidenfeld & Nicolson, 1975.

Thompson, Paul, *The Voice of the Past: Oral History*, Oxford: Oxford University Press, 1978.

Travers, Pauric, 'There was nothing for me there: Irish female emigration, 1922–71', in Patrick O' Sullivan (ed.), *The Irish World Wide, Volume 4: Irish Women and Irish Migration*, 1995, pp. 146–167.

Travers, Pauric, 'Emigration and Gender: The Case of Ireland, 1922–60', in Mary O' Dowd and Sabine Wichert (eds), *Chattel, Servant or Citizen*, 1995, pp. 187–199.

Vaughan, W. E. and Fitzpatrick, A. J. (eds), *Irish Historical Statistics: Population 1821–1971*, Dublin: Royal Irish Academy, 1978.

Wall, Rita, *Leading Lives: Irish Women in Britain*, Dublin: Attic Press, 1991.

Walter, Bronwen, 'Gender and recent Irish migration to Britain', in R. King (ed.), *Contemporary Irish Migration*, 1991, pp. 11–19.

Walter, Bronwen, 'Irishness, gender and place', *Environment and Planning D: Society and Space*, 1995, vol. 13, pp. 35–50.

Walvin, James, *Passage to Britain: Immigration in British History and Politics*, Harmondsworth, Middlesex.: Penguin Books Ltd, 1984.

Ward, Margaret, *The Missing Sex: Putting Women into Irish History*, Dublin: Attic Press, 1991.

Index

Occasional Papers from the Centre for North-West Regional Studies

The Centre for North-West Regional Studies, based at Lancaster University, brings together members of the university and the regional community. As well as its extensive publication programme of books and resourse papers, it organises conferences, study days and seminars covering a wide range of subjects. For a small annual subscription 'Friends of the Centre' receive regular mailings of events and discounts on books and other activities.

For further details contact Centre for North-West Regional Studies, Fylde College, Lancaster University, Lancaster, LA1 4YF; tel: 01524 593770; fax: 01524 594725; email: christine.wilkinson@lancaster.ac.uk; Web site: www.lancs.ac.uk/users/cnwrs.

The Arts and Crafts Movement in the Lake District, 2001, Jennie Brunton	£10.95
Hadrian's Wall: A Social and Cultural History, 2000, Alison Ewin	£8.50
Furness Abbey: Romance, Scholarship and Culture, 2000, C. Dade-Robertson	£11.50
Rural Industries of the Lune Valley, 2000, Michael Winstanley	£9.95
The Romans at Ribchester, 2000, B. J. N. Edwards	£8.95
The Buildings of Georgian Lancaster (revised edition), 2000, Andrew White	£6.95
A History of Linen in the North West, 1998, ed. Elizabeth Roberts	£6.95
History of Catholicism in the Furness Peninsula, 1998, Anne C. Parkinson	£6.95
Vikings in the North West – The Artifacts, 1998, B. J. N. Edwards	£6.95
Sharpe, Paley and Austin, A Lancaster Architectural Practice 1836–1952, 1998, James Price	£6.95
Romans and Britons in Northern England (revised edition), 1997, David Shotter	£6.95
Victorian Terraced Housing in Lancaster, 1996, Andrew White and Mike Winstanley	£6.95
Walking Roman Roads in the Fylde and the Ribble Valley, 1996, Philip Graystone	£5.95
Romans in Lunesdale, 1995, David Shotter and Andrew White	£6.50
Roman Route Across the Northern Lake District, Brougham to Moresby, 1994, Martin Allan	£5.95
Walking Roman Roads in East Cumbria, 1994, Philip Graystone	£5.95
St Martin's College, Lancaster, 1964–89, 1993, Peter S. Gedge and Lois M. R. Louden	£5.95
From Lancaster to the Lakes: the Region in Literature, 1992, eds Keith Hanley and Alison Millbank	£5.95
Windermere in the Nineteenth Century, 1991, ed. Oliver M. Westall	£4.95
Grand Fashionable Nights: Kendal Theatre, 1989, Margaret Eddershaw	£3.95
Rural Life in South West Lancashire, 1988, Alistair Mutch	£3.95
The Diary of William Fisher of Barrow, 1986, eds William Rollinson and Brett Harrison	£2.95
Richard Marsden and the Preston Chartists, 1981, J. E. King	£2.95

Each of these titles may be ordered by post from the above address, postage and packing £1.00 per order. Please make cheques payable to 'The University of Lancaster'. Titles are also available from all good booksellers in the region.